Live PURE and FREE

THE 90-DAY GAME CHANGER

DAVE HOWE

TRISTAN Publishing

Minneapolis

Library of Congress Cataloging-in-Publication Data
Names: Howe, Dave (Founder of Live Pure Ministries), author.
Title: Live pure and free / written by Dave Howe.
Description: Minneapolis : TRISTAN Publishing, 2017.
Identifiers: LCCN 2017024601 | ISBN 9781939881168 (alk. paper)
Subjects: LCSH: Sex addiction—Religious aspects—Christianity. |
Christian men—Sexual behavior. | Christian men—Prayers and devotions.
Classification: LCC BV4627.L8 H69 2017 | DDC 241/.664—dc23 LC record
available at https://lccn.loc.gov/2017024601

Unless otherwise noted, Scripture quotations are from the ESV® Bible (The Holy Bible, English Standard Version®), copyright © 2001 by Crossway, a publishing ministry of Good News Publishers. Used by permission. All rights reserved.

Scripture quotations marked (NIV) are taken from THE HOLY BIBLE, NEW INTERNATIONAL VERSION®, NIV® Copyright © 1973, 1978, 1984, 2011 by Biblica, Inc.® Used by permission. All rights reserved worldwide.

Scripture quotations marked (NLT) are taken from the Holy Bible, New Living Translation, copyright © 1996, 2004, 2007 by Tyndale House Foundation. Used by permission of Tyndale House Publishers, Inc., Carol Stream, Illinois 60188. All rights reserved.

Scripture quotations marked (MSG) are taken from *The Message*. Copyright © 1993, 1994, 1995, 1996, 2000, 2001, 2002. Used by permission of NavPress Publishing Group.

TRISTAN Publishing, Inc.
2355 Louisiana Avenue North
Golden Valley, MN 55427

Copyright © 2017, Dave J. Howe
ISBN 978-1-939881-16-8
First Printing
Printed in Canada

Cover and interior design: Thinkpen Design
Author photo: Adam Bettcher

The anecdotes included in this devotional are a combination of my own experiences and those of a composite of the many men who have participated in my groups over the years. To ensure privacy, names in the stories have been changed, with the exception of those used by permission. Any other similarities to a particular man are purely coincidental.

My experience in leading men's purity groups is as a lay leader, and not as a professional counselor or pastor. While I pray that this book will help you along your purity journey, I also encourage you to consult with a Christian counselor and a pastor as you seek purity.

To learn about all of our books with a message, please visit www.TRISTANpublishing.com.

Dedication

This book is dedicated
to my wife, Barb, the love
of my life, fellow writer,
and my great encourager.
When I asked her who
she thought this book
was for she said,
"Any man with a pulse!"

First Steps Toward Freedom

*We demolish arguments and every pretension that sets
itself up against the knowledge of God, and we take captive
every thought to make it obedient to Christ.*

2 CORINTHIANS 10:5, NIV

I am a man who was trapped in sexual sin and then set free by Christ. Through the grace of God I was released, and I have a passion to lead other men to that same freedom. I am so grateful for God's forgiveness and for His clear demonstration of love for me. I just can't keep it to myself. I want every guy who walks through the doors of the church to experience that same freedom from lust that I now get to experience. When I say every guy who walks through the doors of the church, I'm including every lay leader, every employee, and every pastor. If you are trapped by sexual sin, I want you to know there is hope for you. I get it. I have been there.

*He has sent me to proclaim freedom for the prisoners and
recovery of sight for the blind, to set the oppressed free.*

LUKE 4:18

*"A certain moneylender had two debtors. One owed five hundred
denarii, and the other fifty. When they could not pay, he cancelled
the debt of both. Now which of them will love him more?"* Simon
answered, *"The one, I suppose, for whom he cancelled the larger
debt."* And he said to him, *"You have judged rightly."*

LUKE 7:41–43

I feel the gratitude of the man with the larger debt, and it motivates me to help other men.

My own sexual history started in a way that seemed innocent enough at the time. It began during my early teen years with magazines and girls. As a young teen I'd ride my bicycle downtown to browse the girly magazines at the newsstand. I'd stay there until the clerk would say, "This isn't the library!" That lust for women continued even after getting married. Checking out other women was a bad habit that often led to my getting jabbed with my wife's elbow. Strip clubs and porn became other ways of indulging in lust. As an adult in the early 2000s, I could see it growing unmanageable when pornography became available in every local movie rental store. This is when my use of pornography escalated, affecting everything. I was living a double life—going to church and Sunday school, but then looking at pornography during the week. The cycle of the double life pushed me away from God, who is the one I needed the most. I became preoccupied with porn and spent my time planning when I could look at it again.

In 2004, four things happened that made it clear the time had come to seek help for my sexual issues.

- We moved across town to be closer to church. As we prayed over our house, it struck me that I did not want to give Satan any place in my new home. I knew in my heart that I would have to get rid of my stash of porn.
- I took part in a 40-day small-group study at church. The focus was spiritual discovery.
- I had a vision of Christ on the cross one morning on my way to work. I was driving in bumper-to-bumper traffic when I saw Jesus on the cross to my right in a field. I had to take a second look. He was still there. I heard—in my spirit, not in an audible voice—"You are busy running to work, but you are not paying enough attention to me."
- One Saturday morning at another church, I attended a men's purity event; it was transformational.

After attending the men's purity event, I made a commitment to change and go through their program. It was called a Purity Platoon. My platoon had ten men, a leader, and a co-leader. We met weekly for six months. It was a confidential group where men shared their stories and checked in with the group each week. Checking in gave us the chance to talk honestly about how the week went—both the failures and the victories. We called each other by phone during the week. I have to say, that was very awkward at first. Coming out of isolation and being honest is difficult. We had a workbook with lessons and homework assignments for each week. As I participated, I really felt that we needed a program like this at my church. There just had to be other men besides me who were trapped deep in this sin. It wasn't easy. Sometimes I didn't think I could give up porn, but the struggle was worth it.

Two long—and ultimately victorious—years later, I co-led our church's first group of just three men. The group has grown over the years to the point that we've needed as many as twelve leaders. Every man whom I have worked with in our group has taught me that God is there waiting to set us free. We need only turn to Him, and He is there waiting with open arms.

THE DRIVE TO WRITE THIS BOOK

After working a decade alongside others who struggle, I wanted to share the insights I had gained—with as many men as possible. It seemed that a book would be the perfect thing. However, knowing that most men don't make time to read, I've put the insights into a daily devotion format so a man can read one day's worth—without feeling guilty that he didn't read a whole chapter. Some anecdotes in the devotions reflect my personal story, but most are a composite of the many men I have gotten to know in our group.

Each day's reading includes a devotion that covers a pertinent issue, along with accompanying scripture. At the end of each devotion is an action item. Sometimes the action item is different for married and single men. The action item will let you personalize each day's devotion and help you to take positive steps toward your sexual integrity.

My prayer is that any doubts you may be having at this point will not keep you from reading this book. I want to encourage you. It can be done. You can be free of sexual sin. Don't allow this sin to keep hold of you any longer. Get started right away, but give yourself grace. You still may fall, but keep getting up. This is a process involving your faithful walk every day.

It is my hope and prayer that these devotions will be life-changing as you journey toward purity in Christ. Give God the glory for every victory you experience. It is by His grace and power that you will be able to change. Really, you will.

Day 1

KILL PRIDE

When pride comes, then comes disgrace, but with the humble is wisdom.

PROVERBS 11:2

I was too proud to admit that I needed help.

So there I was, binging on pornography and then purging it. During every purging cycle, I swore I would never do it again. Sure, I had tried and failed before . . . but this time would be different.

I was too proud to ask for help.

I kept on binging and purging. I attended church every Sunday, loved God, and participated in Bible studies regularly. Still, even when help was presented to me, I was too proud to take it.

Pride is just saying, "I can do it all—even the things that only God can do." Pride is putting myself before God. Was I trying to make it look as if I never sinned? Romans 3:23 says, "For all have sinned and fall short of the glory of God." Not some—but all, meaning 100% and without exception. Pride got in the way of my admitting that I am a sinner. But no more.

I am no longer too proud to ask for help with my purity. It is too important an issue just to let it drift. This is no time for DIY thinking. I may still be too proud to ask for directions when driving my truck, but purity is more important than that. I have humbled myself and put aside all my foolish pride. I pray you will too.

PRAY

Lord, help me to be humble and realize that you are the powerful one, not me. Help me to focus on my purity this year and to keep pride from creeping back in. When I experience victory, help me to give you the glory instead of myself.

TAKE ACTION—MARRIED OR SINGLE MAN

List five times pride has gotten in the way for you. What were the results?

Pride	*Results*
fall 2017	fell back into porn
when I got pulled over	a speeding ticket
when I touched Maddie w/o her consent	relationship damage
when I skipped class a lot	got lower grades
when I told Elliot I drank	seen as sinner by him

Be humble and commit to the process. It will take time. There are no exceptions to this rule. Plan out ways that you will guard against pride creeping back in and ruining your purity.

Once I am clean, I will thank God every single day for making me clean. Along the process, I will humble myself to read and write in this stupid book or any other material that can help me.

Day 2

TEMPTATIONS ARE COMMON

No temptation has overtaken you that is not common to man. God is faithful, and he will not let you be tempted beyond your ability, but with the temptation he will also provide the way of escape, that you may be able to endure it.

1 CORINTHIANS 10:13

"But you don't know how things have been for me!"

"I've tried, and I just can't resist."

"Some guys can get victory over this, but my temptations must be worse than theirs."

"They must not have *really* been addicted."

I have listened to men making these excuses for giving in to temptation. For me, temptations of sexual sin have seemed so huge. In fact, for years I thought they were beyond defeat. In my isolation, the burden and shame of the sins have weighed so heavily on me. Isolation reinforced my sense that I was defeated and there was no saving me from the dark place I was in. My temptation seemed heavier than what everyone else experienced.

However, God says that my temptation is not unique, and it is even common. He also says it can be overcome. My temptations are no worse than any other guy's. What a relief to know that we are not abandoned and that God is not allowing us to be overcome by sin.

PRAY

Lord, it is comforting to know my temptations
are not unique to me, but common to all men.
This gives me hope for the future. You really are
making a way for me to stay close to you. Still, I will
need your strength and continued grace to win,
because I cannot stay away from sin on my own.

TAKE ACTION—MARRIED OR SINGLE MAN

Recall the dark place where you were at your worst. Aren't you glad to know that your temptations are common and that God always provides a way out? What a great and loving God we follow!

List five specific things that give you hope as you start to overcome temptation.

1. My parents
2. My future wife
3. My Friends at Wheaton
4. Derek
5. Caleb

What are the three things that help you the most to stay pure?

1. This book
2. prayer
3. the Bible

Day 3

LUST CHECKED

For everything in the world—the lust of the flesh, the lust of the eyes,
and the pride of life—comes not from the Father but from the world.
1 JOHN 2:16, NIV

The sexual images of women that have come from pornography are etched into my brain because of the very way that God created our brains. Regrettably, the imprint on my brain that God intended for the image of my wife has been perverted toward the women in porn videos.

When I repented of my sexual sin, in order to get a check on lust immediately, I consciously chose to start looking at women differently. I began to view older women like moms. I changed my perspective of women who are about my age to be like sisters. Younger women and girls I now see as daughters. If I see them as daughters, I will see myself in a father role with young women—as their protector.

Looking at women in this new way disrupts the lustful thought pattern completely, which helps me stay pure in my thoughts. This newfound viewpoint allows me to look innocently at women again. Christian women are my sisters in the Lord.

Now I look at my wife as the only woman for me and the only woman I will focus on sexually. God gave me a wonderful woman to love, and I will continue to focus all my sexual attention on her alone.

PRAY

Thank you, Lord, for the women in my life. Guide me
to see women always in a respectful way, in a way that
honors them as your beautiful creations. Help me to
honor my wife by giving her all of my attention and love.

TAKE ACTION—MARRIED OR SINGLE MAN

What are some more ways that you can avoid looking at women in a lustful way?

MEMORIZE PHILIPPIANS 1:6 *And I am sure of this, that he who began a good work in you will bring it to completion at the day of Jesus Christ.*

MEMORIZE 1 CORINTHIANS 10:13 *No temptation has overtaken you that is not common to man. God is faithful, and he will not let you be tempted beyond your ability, but with the temptation he will also provide the way of escape, that you may be able to endure it.*

Start looking at women in this new way and disrupt lustful thought patterns. Once you stop lusting after women during the day, your nights will get easier; and it will be easier to stay away from porn. You have to stop looking at porn to stop putting those images into your head. The images will fade over time when you stop the lust cycle. Fill your head with verses of scripture and praise songs, which will help you in renewing your mind.

MARRIED MAN

What nice things can you do today to show your wife that she is appreciated and that you love her and no other? List at least five.

1.

2.

3.

4.

5.

Day 4

STOP WASTING TIME

*But I say to you that everyone who looks at a woman with lustful
intent has already committed adultery with her in his heart.*

MATTHEW 5:28

Through the years, no matter how much fun I thought I was having watching pornography, the Holy Spirit has never left me alone. Even in the midst of my sin, I felt His presence, and heard Him in my heart. *You're wasting time. You're wasting valuable time. You'll never get this time back. There are so many important things I want you to be doing.*

The Holy Spirit was always after me.

And when I finally started listening to Him—being obedient—each day that I stayed away from porn, I grew more involved with my family. I used my time more wisely. What joy! Besides my family, I was connecting again with friends and neighbors. A watershed moment for me occurred one sunny afternoon as I worked in my home office. Looking out the window from my desk, I noticed my neighbor and his son digging a drain trench. My immediate thought: *I am going to go out there to give them a hand.*

Now, this was not a typical reaction for me, and I suddenly realized that I was turning away from my focus on myself and toward an interest in helping those around me. In that precious moment, God gave me a sign that I was healing.

I have one life to live, and I am going to live it for His glory!

PRAY

Lord, I am sorry for all the time that I wasted. Thank you for continuing to love me through this process of turning away from my sexual sins. I love you, and I will devote my time to giving you glory and living for you. You are worthy.

TAKE ACTION—MARRIED OR SINGLE MAN

Because you know that pornography has been wasting your time . . . Whom would you like to help?

My parents, brother, friends

Which goals have you not yet accomplished because of all the time wasted?

Better grades, not in a relationship

List positive hobbies that you have put on the shelf because you never get around to them.

Piano playing, billiards, movie watching

How can you get more involved in your church and your community for the glory of God?

to actually regularly attend a church.

Day 5

BOAT DANCING

*God, the Lord, is my strength; he makes my feet like
the deer's; he makes me tread on my high places.*

HABAKKUK 3:19

There is an old Irish proverb that goes like this: "God is good—but never dance in a small boat." I can relate to this Irish proverb because it requires action on my part—and responsible action. God is good, and He wants to help, and He wants my success. I have to act in a reasonable manner. I have to take action to invite God to work in my life, and for me to show my reliance on—and my faith in—Him.

I now know that I can't stay up late after everyone else has gone to bed, surfing the internet "just looking around" and being "curious," and then wondering why I started looking at porn again. That is like dancing in a small boat and expecting that it won't capsize. I would be setting myself up for failure and expecting God to save me. That would be an unreasonable expectation on my part.

Getting pure is not a cakewalk, but I must avoid making it harder than it needs to be. It is a battle, and I have my part to do. I need a strategy, and I have to carry it out.

It is a battle that can be won. Not because of my strength, but by the grace and power of Christ, our Lord. I can't sit on the internet wandering around and expecting not to fall.

PRAY

Lord, help me to take action to show that I am reliant on
you and have full faith in you. Help me to understand that
I have an active role to play in my quest for purity. I cannot
act irresponsibly and still expect my boat not to capsize.

TAKE ACTION—MARRIED OR SINGLE MAN

It's important that you understand this quickly. You have to be smart about this battle and put all safety measures in place to get you through this change in your life. The beginning is the hardest because your habits are likely to be very entrenched. Don't waste any time telling yourself that you don't need this measure or that precaution—you do.

How have you been trying to dance in a small boat and expecting it never to capsize?

List three reasonable steps you can take to stay pure.

1. _always leave my phone away from my bed_
2. _fricken sleep on my back even thaugh it's hard_
3. _Call someone when I'm turned on and talk about anything_

Make a commitment that you will do whatever it takes to create an environment for success. Admit to the Lord that on your own you can't do this, but with Him all things are possible.

"But Jesus looked at them and said, 'With man this is impossible, but with God all things are possible'" (Matthew 19:26).

Make a schedule for your nighttime routine. Include Bible study time, and turn off all electronics at least a half hour before you go to bed. This will help you to relax and rest well. Set a reasonable time to retire every night. Try texting your accountability partner when you are ready to go to sleep. That extra piece of accountability can help you stay on track.

turn off electronics, read, get in bed, lay on back, drink cherry juice. I cannot set a regular, reasonable time. Think while laying on back often memes of wholesome pictures.

Day 6

MY CHURCH REPUTATION

For all have sinned and fall short of the glory of God.

ROMANS 3:23

There is only one perfect person in the Bible. The people who claimed to be perfect were the ones Jesus pointed out as hypocrites. They were outwardly righteous and followed all the rules, but their hearts were not following after God.

I now realize that following Christ is more important than anything else. I am honest about my struggles, and I try not to manipulate what people at church think about me by putting on a false front and pretending I don't have any problems.

Trying to look like I'm perfect is just vanity and dishonesty, anyway. We are all sinners.

Interestingly, more than half of the men who attend purity groups do so at churches other than their own because they worry about their reputations at their own churches.

I remember when Jeff first came to our small group. He was so worried that he'd see someone he knew since he had grown up in the city where the meeting was being held. Sure enough, a good friend of his, Jon—who also had grown up in that same city—was there. Rather than shaming Jeff, Jon welcomed him and said he was glad to see his friend, that they could work on their purity together. Both of these men are now leading purity groups at their own churches in different parts of town.

Don't worry about your reputation at church.

PRAY

Lord, I want to follow you and be obedient to your commands. You say your yoke is easy. Help me not to focus on what I think people will think. I long to be close to you and grow in my love for you. Help me to be humble and to put away my pride.

TAKE ACTION—MARRIED OR SINGLE MAN

Some things, like reputation, feel as if they are in the way of making changes in our lives. They are blocks in our minds that can be removed.

Describe a time when you wanted to do something but you had a list of potential barriers. Which of these anticipated barriers never happened, or were not a big deal?

Nothing comes to mind.

Don't let concerns about your reputation keep you from facing your sexual addiction and getting help. God might have a plan for you to be a future leader like Jon and Jeff.

Day 7

STASH REMOVAL

*But among you there must not be even a hint of sexual
immorality, or of any kind of impurity, or of greed,
because these are improper for God's holy people.*

EPHESIANS 5:3, NIV

Early in my addiction to porn, I would buy tapes or DVDs, view them, and then destroy them. I vowed that this would be the last time I would ever look at porn. But it was not the last time. At some point later—a week, a month, two months—I would buy another one. The cycle of guilt, shame, and repentance happened again and again.

But then something different began to happen. I started to save an occasional DVD. This progressed until there was a collection, a stash. I hung on to my stash until I went to my first group meeting. We were told that our assignment was to get rid of everything that was part of our sexual sin collection.

My concern had been that someone would find videos or magazines, and my sin would be exposed. I had been hesitant to invite people over to our house because of it. But now I can invite anyone to look anywhere, and it is all safe. What a freeing experience! The Devil no longer has a foothold in my home—or anywhere in my life.

As part of my changed life, I got rid of my stash of pornography: favorite sites, pictures, and everything that fed my addiction. My house, car, computer, electronic gadgets, garage—it's all clean!

PRAY

Thank you, Lord, for loving me and helping me as I continue on the road to becoming the man you want me to be. I am succeeding with your strength and your grace. Strengthen me to never look back, but to press ever forward.

TAKE ACTION—MARRIED OR SINGLE MAN

Have you gotten rid of your stash yet? Now is the time to purge it all. Yes, even the one you may be thinking about keeping. Everything has to go. Absolutely everything. You don't want Satan to have any stronghold in your life.

I've had men in my small groups who saved one thing—just one—and they eventually fell because of it. Cleaning your house, your whole life—and cleaning it completely—will give you your first glimpse of freedom. It is also a tangible commitment to purity in your life; your line in the sand. *Not in my house!*

Day 8

JESUS OVERCAME

And he (Satan) said to him, "All these I will give you, if you will fall down and worship me." Then Jesus said to him, "Be gone, Satan! For it is written, 'You shall worship the Lord your God and him only shall you serve.'"

MATTHEW 4:9–10

Resisting temptation is possible. Jesus was tempted by the Devil in the desert when He was hungry and thirsty after forty days of fasting.

"Those who belong to Christ Jesus have crucified the flesh with its passions and desires" (Galatians 5:24). Because of this, I am no longer a slave to sin. Jesus said in His Word that He would provide a way out so that we can endure it when we are tempted.

It is comforting to know that I follow a God who came to earth and became a man, fully God and fully man. He has endured all the temptations that I face in my own life. He both understands me and cares about me.

PRAY

Thank you, Lord, for your example of resisting temptation. You used the Scripture to rebuke Satan, and I can too. I can resist temptation with your strength.

TAKE ACTION—MARRIED OR SINGLE MAN

How has God provided a way out for you recently?

Sent people into the room

Are there any temptations you think you cannot resist?

nope

Make a plan right now for when each of these temptations occurs. Be prepared before the temptation arises.

Temptation	Plan

Day 9

ARMOR IN PLACE

*Put on the whole armor of God, that you may be able to stand against the
schemes of the devil. For we do not wrestle against flesh and blood, but
against the rulers, against the authorities, against the cosmic powers over
this present darkness, against the spiritual forces of evil in the heavenly
places. Therefore, take up the whole armor of God, that you may be able to
withstand in the evil day, and having done all, to stand firm. Stand therefore,
having fastened on the belt of truth, and having put on the breastplate of
righteousness, and, as shoes for your feet, having put on the readiness given
by the gospel of peace. In all circumstances take up the shield of faith, with
which you can extinguish all the flaming darts of the evil one; and take the
helmet of salvation, and the sword of the Spirit, which is the word of God.*

EPHESIANS 6:11–17

As I step out into the world each day, I will face temptations and distractions of many kinds. In the past, I was swept away by them. I was an easy target. "Your adversary the devil prowls around like a roaring lion, seeking someone to devour" (1 Peter 5:8). The problem was not all external either; my mind is an idol factory. By idol factory I mean that my mind is able to put so many things higher than God, making them idols in my life. Things like money, cars, boats, porn, and lust were all idols.

It is naive of me to think that I can go into the day as a fully devoted follower of Christ without being properly prepared. I must put on the full armor of God as spelled out in Ephesians 6:11–17. Spending time in the Word and in prayer every day helps to focus me in the way I need to go.

PRAY

Lord, thank you for spelling out the full armor for me.
I need it. Help me to diligently prepare myself each day,
and then carry out my day your way, in your power.

TAKE ACTION—MARRIED OR SINGLE MAN

Write out what your routine will be for preparing your day with the full armor. Schedule it on your calendar to make it real.

_____

_____

_____

_____

As you put this routine into action, journal about how preparing your day in this way makes a difference in your life. Does it help you resist temptations? If so, how?

_____

_____

_____

Keep a journal of your purity journey. Include both struggles and triumphs. Journaling has been proven to engage a different part of your brain. It can help you to clarify the changes and healing you will be experiencing. Read _Journaling_ in the Appendix for more information on the benefits, along with suggestions on how to begin.

Day 10

A GUARDED HEART

Turn my eyes from looking at worthless things; and give me life in your ways.

PSALM 119:37

There is always more out there. For years I was always looking for the next new toy to add to my collection so I could feel that buzz of excitement. Toys were things like cars, boats, dream homes, ATVs, jet skis, and real estate. Maybe it was the next great meal at the new restaurant. I wasn't guarding my heart with the peace of God. Instead, my mind—the idol factory—was producing more counterfeit gods.

And then there were the women and the unfaithfulness to my wife that I exhibited by my flirting with the women at the office and looking at porn. With these idols I covered up my anxieties about work, home, and the pains of the past. I remember a former co-worker saying that he was always "falling in love" with women. He was married, but he was not guarding his heart and keeping it focused on his wife. Neither was I.

There is no need to keep covering up my anxieties about today and the pains of the past. The anxieties and the pain can be turned over to God in prayer. He has all I need, and there is no reason to keep searching out substitutes for His love. I am a citizen of heaven, and I can have victory over sin. The peace He gives will be the guardian of my heart and mind in Christ.

PRAY

Lord, you are all-sufficient. I focus my heart first on you. Thank you for your love and protection. Help me be alert to guarding my heart and remembering that the things of the world will never satisfy.

TAKE ACTION—MARRIED OR SINGLE MAN

What things, people, or even goals are taking your heart from what should be the Lord's? List them.

_____

_____

_____

_____

Are you guarding your heart? If so, how do you do it? If not, how can you start?

_____

_____

_____

Reflect on this verse: "But seek first the kingdom of God and his righteousness, and all these things will be added to you" (Matthew 6:33). How does the message of this verse fit into your plan to guard your heart?

List five steps you can take to guard your heart.

1. _____

2. _____

3. _____

4. _____

5. _____

Day 11

CAREFUL LIVING

Be very careful, then, how you live—not as unwise but as wise, making the most of every opportunity, because the days are evil. Therefore do not be foolish, but understand what the Lord's will is. Do not get drunk on wine, which leads to debauchery. Instead, be filled with the Spirit, speaking to one another with psalms, hymns, and songs from the Spirit. Sing and make music from your heart to the Lord, always giving thanks to God the Father for everything, in the name of our Lord Jesus Christ.

EPHESIANS 5:15–20, NIV

I spent many days of my life not being careful how I lived. I spent many hours viewing vile pornography and wasting precious hours of my life. My Friday farewell to co-workers revealed a lot. "Have a good weekend! Don't do anything I wouldn't do; and that leaves you a lot of room!"

In those days, whatever happened, I would flow with it. The Bible was not my guide. I thought nothing of going into bad neighborhoods to hang out at strip clubs.

I now recognize the precious life that God has given me. I am learning to be more and more careful of the manner in which I live, conscious of my surroundings.

On the computer I do what I need to do, and then log off and join my family. No more kidding myself that I am "just researching" and need to spend hours on the computer every day. I will be *present* with my family.

PRAY

Lord, I want to serve you. All the distractions of the world combined do not add up to the wonder of knowing you. Thank you for helping me to focus on you. Help me to live my life in the *present,* being careful how I live.

TAKE ACTION—MARRIED OR SINGLE MAN

If you are like I was—and like so many of the men in the small groups I've led, you have been living an undisciplined and selfish lifestyle. If so, you need some structure to change this. To add structure, plan how you will manage your time on the computer each night of the week and for the weekends. Share the plan with your wife, if you are married.

Remember to plan out how you will handle Christmas vacation and any other long holiday periods, including three-day holiday weekends. I've put together a guideline for you called the *Purity Protection Plan*. You'll find it in the Appendix at the back of the book.

As you start to execute your plan, make any necessary changes to be sure your plan is workable. If you are married, build your plan with your wife so there are enough safeguards in place to make her feel safe. You are in the process of building trust. As your healing progresses, you may want to loosen some of the restrictions of the plan. For example, at some point you may feel that you can use certain apps that you got into trouble with in the past. Discuss these ideas with your wife. If she does not agree, keep the restrictions in place.

If you want to break the porn addiction, then a life of doing whatever you want, whenever you want to, has to end.

Find an accountability partner—a man you can trust to listen and support your process of turning away from sexual sin.

To learn more, read *Accountability Partner* in the Appendix.

Day 12

WANTED: PURE MAN

Let marriage be held in honor among all, and let the marriage bed be
undefiled, for God will judge the sexually immoral and adulterous.

HEBREWS 13:4

It's not that bad, I told myself. *It's not hurting anyone, and I enjoy the escape.*
I don't want to give this up forever. I don't know that I even could.

My self-justifying thoughts weren't something that even I could believe
after a while. And part of the reason for that was an important question:
would my wife really appreciate it if I went to the trouble of completely
quitting porn? Of course she would. The answer was obvious, but not easy
to admit—even to myself.

Even so, her feelings were a huge factor in my commitment to getting
pure, both because I want to do what God wants, and because I had made a
vow to my wife on our wedding day to be faithful, forsaking all others. She
married me with the understanding that I would love her—and her only.
Loving my wife does not include making her compete with women in strip
clubs or porn videos—or any other women. My wife needed me back on an
exclusive basis. I promised her that before God.

So, would your wife—or future wife if you're single—appreciate it if you'd
quit? The answer is a resounding "Yes!" It will be hard to quit—as hard as
quitting alcohol or cigarettes—and maybe harder. After all, using pornography is an addiction too. But quitting will be worth it.

PRAY

Lord, thank you for drawing me closer to you and opening my eyes
about how this sin has impacted my life. I am sorry for sinning against
you with my porn viewing and other sexual sins. Help me to replace
my vile habits with habits that honor you and my loved ones. I am
committed to purity, and I know that I can be pure only with your power.

TAKE ACTION—MARRIED MAN

Sometimes a man has come to one of my small groups only because he was given an ultimatum by his wife. He has joined the group only because of outside pressure. However, it is not until a man decides for himself that he needs to change, that change will be possible. You must be committed to it yourself.

What was the determining factor that made you start your purity journey?

My mom catching me

What has made you commit to it?

My mom

What are some of the ways you can continue to show your wife how important she is to you and how you have recommitted to honoring your marriage vows?

SINGLE MAN

Congratulations on committing to be pure for the sake of your own manhood! What was the determining factor that got you started on your purity journey?

What has made you commit to it?

Women dream about marrying a pure man. Imagine blessing her by already being pure before your journey together even begins. If you do marry someday, your wife will be blessed that you are finding your purity in Christ now.

Day 13

COMPUTER BAR

Keep your heart with all vigilance, for from it flow the springs of life.
PROVERBS 4:23

Hours spent at the computer viewing porn late at night are over. That habit has long been ingrained in my brain; however, I realize it must be broken for me to develop healthy habits.

I am on a new path to purity. I have accountability partners, and I have accountability software on my computer. My computer screen is visible to the doorway of my office. If needed, I will have my accountability partners take my laptop for a while to get the temptation away from me.

I know I cannot go to my "bar" every night and sit there white-knuckling it, hoping I will not fall. This would be like an alcoholic going to a bar every night and thinking he won't have a drink. That is foolishness. I have to be smart about this and take simple steps to help myself.

I may need to move my computer to the living room where all can see. I will teach my wife how to check the history of my web searches. I can also make a password protection that only my wife knows so I can be on the computer only with her awareness.

PRAY

Lord, help me to go about getting pure with my mind alert. Help me to see the obvious precautions I must take and give me the strength to take those steps. Help me to "come to my senses" as the prodigal son did. Thank you for loving me through this.

TAKE ACTION—MARRIED OR SINGLE MAN

Be aware that once you have viewed porn online, porn sites can track you and advertise to you as well as put malicious adware on your computer. The porn industry is aggressive about keeping you as a customer. I suggest taking your machine to a repair shop and having it scanned for malware. It may be necessary to perform a system restore or a factory reset.

Put accountability software like Covenant Eyes on your computer and all the smart phones, tablets, and laptops in the house. See *Accountability Software* in the Appendix for more about this topic.

You can have your accountability partner checking your software reports daily at first. It might be best to completely stay away from the TV, computer, tablet, and smartphone while you are home alone. This can help give you a little breathing room in your effort to change your habits.

Your electronic devices and software applications have helpful features like parental control and internet access time limits. Use their features like guardrails to help yourself stay on the road to purity.

You have to get more than assertive. You have to get aggressive. And whatever you do, keep that newly cleaned computer clean.

Make a list of things you can start doing right now to help protect yourself. If you think of your electronic devices as the equivalent of a bar for an alcoholic, what can you do to stay out of the "bar" and away from what feeds your addiction?

_____

_____

_____

_____

Day 14

GRACE TRAINING

For the grace of God has appeared, bringing salvation for all people, training us to renounce ungodliness and worldly passions, and to live self-controlled, upright, and godly lives in the present age.

TITUS 2:11–12

In my darkest days, I did not hear that there was grace for me—if I would have just turned to the Lord for help. I felt ashamed and unworthy of any nice treatment from God—or anyone else, for that matter.

I struggled with allowing God to show me grace. I kept thinking that I could do this on my own, and I wanted to manage everything and keep God at a distance. I thought maybe, once I was cleaned up, I would ask God for support. How foolish I was. I had no ability to clean myself up. And God does not want to be kept at a distance. When I finally turned to Him, He was right there, close by, with grace.

God is like the father in the story of the prodigal son. Even though the son did terrible things, including sexual sin with prostitutes, the father still loved him and was always on the lookout for his homecoming. The father still loved his son with an unconditional love.

In the same way, our heavenly Father loves me, and He still wanted to show me His grace and mercy—even as I turned away from Him in sexual sin. He was waiting expectantly for me too.

I finally accepted His gift of grace. Now I know I can live a self-controlled and godly life.

Lord, you are so wonderful! You have given me everything I need!

PRAY

Father, please help me by opening my eyes to see, and my heart to accept, what you have already done. Your grace is beyond my human imagination. I am so grateful to you for loving me that much. Where would I be today without your grace? Help me now to renounce the ungodliness and worldly passions and to live in a self-controlled way.

TAKE ACTION—MARRIED OR SINGLE MAN

Write out some examples of when you have experienced grace in your life.

_____

_____

List how you have shown grace to those closest to you.

_____

_____

Have you opened yourself up to the grace God has for you to help you with your purity? If so, explain how. If not, what seems to be holding you back?

_____

_____

_____

Remember, He is there, just waiting for you.

Day 15

ACCOUNTABILITY IS NEEDED

Without counsel plans fail, but with many advisers they succeed.

PROVERBS 15:22

This sin had driven me more and more into isolation. It was refreshing, although awkward, to have accountability partners; but I began making phone calls to them regularly. Their encouragement has been critical to the changes I'm going through on the road to purity, a critical part of my journey to eliminate habitual behaviors.

By being open and honest with my accountability partners and talking to them often, I can—with God's help—break the sinful habits. I had been protecting and hiding these habits, but I will no longer keep them under cover. For when they are out in the open, they lose their power over me.

Alone I was defeated, but together with others I can be victorious.

PRAY

Thank you for giving me male companions for the journey. Help me to be open and honest. Break the arrogant attitude I have had about being independent. I don't want to be about me anymore. I want to be about you, Lord. Thank you for the grace you have shown me. Let me show that grace to others.

TAKE ACTION—MARRIED OR SINGLE MAN

Open up with your accountability partner. Contact him today with the purpose of getting to know him better. Begin to develop a view of your relationship as lifelong. You have shared—and will continue to share—very private aspects of your life with him, and you will want to continue that relationship. You will always need a place to share sexual issues with a man who understands you. You will want to be surrounded by men who, like King David, are after God's own heart. As Christians, we were not meant to operate on our own. Know that we experience God in a special way when we experience Him with a brother in the Lord.

Are there hobbies you would like to start—or ones that you and your accountability partner have in common? What are they? List them here. Arrange your calendar so you can meet weekly at a set time with your partner.

To learn more, read *Accountability Partner* in the Appendix.

Day 16

LET IT GO

If you forgive others their trespasses,
your heavenly Father will also forgive you.

MATTHEW 6:14

I was mad about the "to do" lists she made for me, mad about raking the yard, mad about cleaning up—you name it, I was mad. Thus, piling up everything that went wrong between my wife and me became a daily activity. I kept a running list, getting angrier as I added each item.

My thoughts toward her became more and more negative. *See, she doesn't understand me.* My grievance list became my admission ticket to watching porn later that night.

Finally, I began to see that list for what it was. It was unforgiveness, along with my creating tension as an excuse to feed the addiction. Feeling sorry for myself was just another excuse for acting out. Both showed a lack of gratitude for the wonderful wife God has given me.

I am learning to let go of all the small disagreements and arguments with my wife. I let it all go! None of it is worth holding on to. I will extend grace and forgiveness to her. Those grievances are not important. We can discuss and resolve issues. I want a healthy relationship with my wife—with no resentment.

PRAY

Lord, you died for our sins and forgave us for
them all. Help me to be quick to forgive and slow
to anger. I ask for a mouth that easily speaks
forgiveness for others and praise for you.

TAKE ACTION—MARRIED OR SINGLE MAN

List the excuses you use to feed your addiction. Next, let it all go. Start each evening with no list of grievances, but with simple gratitude for your day, and write down that list. Post it where you can see it daily, and add to it often.

Day 17

FEARLESS LIVING

For God gave us a spirit not of fear but of power and love and self-control.
2 TIMOTHY 1:7

As a child, I had good reason to fear. My parents loved me, yet they often made me afraid. It seemed that life spun out of control, not as it should be or how I wanted it to be. My emotional needs were left wanting because my parents were unable to meet them. Mom and Dad were trying to work out their own issues.

Other men from my small groups have described abuse from parents and stepparents. It left them fearful. It makes sense for a scared young boy to look for relief from the fear and to seek pleasure wherever he could find it.

As I heal from the sexual addiction, it's the right time to discover if I'm still operating in the fear mode of my youth. Understanding the fear helps me to steer clear of sexual sin.

Facing my fears and resisting my tendency to hide helps to reveal that there is truly nothing to be afraid of. God's Word encourages me that "I can do all things through him who strengthens me" (Philippians 4:13).

PRAY

Lord, help me to live out a fearless lifestyle. Help me to trust you and gain a spirit of power and love. Help me not to be afraid as I face life and remember that I can do all things through you.

TAKE ACTION—MARRIED OR SINGLE MAN

The question is this: are you operating out of fear?

List three key decisions you made last month. Were any of these decisions affected by fear? In those cases, how may your decisions have differed had you been fearless?

Decision #1

Fear

Fear's Effect on Decision

Fearless Decision

Decision #2

Fear

Fear's Effect on Decision

Fearless Decision

Decision #3

Fear

Fear's Effect on Decision

Fearless Decision

Start to live the fearless life now!

Day 18

ALONE NO MORE

For he has said, I will never leave you nor forsake you.

HEBREWS 13:5

When I was a child, hiding and isolating myself made sense for my own physical and emotional safety. I could not control the angry adults, and I wanted to avoid getting into the middle of the yelling and screaming. It frightened me, as well it should any child. However, the result has been long lasting. Withdrawing from the chaos caused me to be a loner emotionally. Being alone to take care of my own emotional needs was the way I learned to live.

As an adult, feeling that I must be the only man with this problem was a barrier to discussing it with anyone. It has been a painful process for me to open up.

I am still emerging from isolation, and my sin is no longer secret. I am talking more than ever with my wife, and we continue growing closer. I am not alone because I am closer to God, relying on His power and His grace.

The Bible says that I should not fear but give thanksgiving and take my needs to God in prayer. With God, my wife, and my church, I am no longer alone.

PRAY

Lord, help me to connect with people and with you. I no longer want to be isolated. You want fellowship with me, and so do the people in my life. I seek the fellowship with you that your Word describes. Help me to break from my old ways of childhood to healthy, adult ways of dealing with issues in my life.

TAKE ACTION—MARRIED OR SINGLE MAN

Did you isolate yourself as a child? As a teen or as a young adult? If so, what was going on in your life that precipitated your isolation?

_____

_____

_____

Are there situations that tend to make you isolate today? If so, list them.

_____

_____

_____

What strategies can you use to avoid isolating yourself? List at least five strategies.

1. _____

2. _____

3. _____

4. _____

5. _____

I encourage you to be in fellowship with other believers. The Lord wants fellowship with you, so stay in the Word and draw close to Him in prayer. Your heart is a house that's not meant to be lived in alone. End the isolation; invite people into your heart by sharing feelings, thoughts, and other aspects of your life.

Day 19

EYE CONTROL

I made a covenant with my eyes not to look lustfully at a young woman.
JOB 31:1, NIV

I allowed my eyes to wander, always checking out women during the day. In the evening, I spent time online or watching movies to keep my eyes on whatever could feed my lust. It was as if my eyes were a mouth, continually feeding my compulsive appetite for lust food.

What a battle it has been to starve that appetite, but—to God's glory—there is no more of that lifestyle for me. Unfortunately, I cannot restrict what the world does, so my eyes will still see things that are tempting to me; but I have learned to move my eyes past these temptations quickly. With God's help, now I can bounce my eyes away from temptation to avoid a second look. Remember, it is not a failure to be tempted. It's what you do with that temptation that matters.

By not giving in to temptation, my eyes are opening up to the beauty of nature and the wonders of God's creation. I see the beauty in a sunset, the beauty of flowers and sunshine, as I have never seen them before. God made my eyes to feed on the beauty of the world—not the sin in this world.

PRAY

Thank you for the gift of sight. Thank you for giving
us such a beautiful world and beautiful stars in the
heavens at night. Lord, help me to be disciplined
about where I look. I want to focus on the beauty
of your creation without any lust in my thoughts.
I want to see things with a pure heart again.

TAKE ACTION—MARRIED OR SINGLE MAN

What are some practical things you can do to avoid looking lustfully at women? Make a list.

_____

_____

_____

_____

_____

_____

What can you do to reduce the visual temptations of your day? Plan a strategy so you are proactive instead of reactive. For example, you may have to plan a different commute route so you don't drive past that one billboard. You may have to walk an alternate route around your office to bypass certain women on the way to your cubicle.

_____

_____

_____

_____

Make a covenant with your eyes like Job did not to look lustfully at young women. Write down that covenant, post it so you can read it daily, and live it out with God's strength. Give God the glory for your victories.

Day 20

EVIL FISHING LURES

We don't want to unwittingly give Satan an opening for yet more mischief—we're not oblivious to his sly ways!

2 CORINTHIANS 2:11, MSG

Early in the addiction, I was unaware of the Devil's ways, and I walked right into many of his traps—like the lies about who I am, and the lies that sexual sin would give more pleasure than saving sex for marriage, the way God intended. Satan is the father of lies. He lied and said that God with all of His rules was just trying to keep me from having fun.

Satan's lies are like fishing lures. As you probably know, a fishing lure has a barb on the end of the hook; and once a fish grabs it, that fish no longer has the choice of letting go.

Indulging in sexual sin is like biting the fishing lure that Satan has cast in your direction. It's shiny and attractive looking; but once you've bitten, you're hooked in the heart with a barb that's hard to remove. So flee sexual immorality before the hook is set in you.

Satan is evil. If you take his lure for sexual sin, he does two things. First, he laughs at you and calls you a weak sucker for falling for his tricks. There is no love or sympathy from the Devil. Keep in mind that he is out to destroy you. He wants to destroy your authority in your family—and to destroy your entire family as a result. He wants to make you ineffective in the church and in the community. He wants you to stay in your sin. He wants you hidden, full of shame, and isolated. Second, he tells you that God doesn't love you anymore because you are a worthless sinner—and that there's no hope for you.

In my process of healing, I have become more aware of the Devil's schemes and lies. Now I reflect on who I am in Christ. I am more than a conqueror. I am forgiven. I am loved. I am a joint heir with Christ.

PRAY

Lord, thank you that your ways are the best ways.
Thank you that your plan for sexuality is not about
taking away my fun, but about protecting me and
guiding me into what is best for me and my family.
Lord, I want to be that effective leader in my house,
my church, and my community. With your strength
and the Holy Spirit's guidance, I will stay away from
immoral behaviors and stay focused on you.

TAKE ACTION—MARRIED OR SINGLE MAN

Be alert to the lies of the Devil and how he attempts to hook into you. Make a
list of the Devil's lies that have caught you off guard in the past. List at least three.

1. _____

2. _____

3. _____

His lure of the temporary pleasure of sexual sin has too high a cost. The
Devil wants to make you ineffective by keeping you ashamed and isolated.
He wants to keep you away from leadership in the church and among your
peers and co-workers. He doesn't want you out evangelizing either. Part
of winning a fight is developing an understanding of your Enemy and his
strategies. Now that you have the knowledge and can better understand
what you're up against, you can win. With God's help, of course.

For each item on your list, answer the following questions: When do you
find the lie particularly tempting? How can you prepare yourself to stand up
to this lie? Which verses can you memorize to help?

Day 21

LORD OF MY LIFE

For as the heavens are higher than the earth, so are my ways higher than your ways and my thoughts than your thoughts.

ISAIAH 55:9

It was easy for me to ask Jesus to be my Savior. It was a free gift, and all I had to do was ask and receive. It took little effort on my part. I did have to admit that I was a sinner and needed forgiveness, which took some courage, but it only took a tiny amount of faith—the size of a mustard seed. I believe that bit of faith was from the Holy Spirit.

Of course, I was also supposed to turn from my sins; but that part of the equation got lost somewhere in the excitement of being saved.

The hard part for me was when the realization hit that I had asked Him not only to be my Savior, but to be the Lord of my life. I had trouble with that concept. *You mean He would be Lord over my finances, my home, my work, my leisure, and yes—my sexuality? Wow. That is a whole different story.*

For Him to be the Lord of my life, I would have to do something . . . and give up some things. I would need to give up calling all the shots. It would have to be His agenda instead of mine.

As unappealing as that was, I knew that I needed to get healed from the sexual addiction . . . and so I needed to be sold out to Christ and turn from my sins 180 degrees. I would have to make Him the Lord of my whole life. It hasn't been easy, but I am using this time of sexual healing to focus on my commitment to be totally obedient to the Lord.

I have to learn to trust Him in everything. I know that on my own I have not been able to defeat the sexual addiction. It's clear to me that I need His supernatural, resurrection power to overcome it. His ways I love. They are higher than my ways. His yoke is so much easier than the sexual-sin hell I had been living in.

PRAY

Thank you, Lord, for loving me even when I was far from you. Help me to surrender more to you every day. Thank you for forgiving all my sins. I want you to be the Lord of my life. Thank you for loving me.

TAKE ACTION—MARRIED OR SINGLE MAN

What were the hardest things for you to turn over to God? List them.

_____

_____

_____

Are you still holding on to something? If so, what is it? In order to break the addiction, you will have to turn over sex to Him.

_____

_____

_____

Do you believe any lies about your sexuality that are holding you back from trusting His way fully? If so, replace that lie with the truth of God. List each lie and its replacement.

_____

_____

_____

Day 22

FEEL THE FEELINGS

"Where have you put him?" he asked them. They told him,
"Lord, come and see." Then Jesus wept. The people who were
standing nearby said, "See how much he loved him!"

JOHN 11:34–36, NLT

I have feelings, and it is okay to have my feelings. I own them, whatever they are. Even though I have stuffed my feelings for many years, I want to start to know them, feel them, and embrace them to better understand myself.

I need to understand my feelings in order to have a healthy sex life and avoid falling into sexual sin again. I also need to express my feelings. No one, and I mean no one, has the right to tell me that I can't feel the way I do.

My mother used to tell me, "You shouldn't feel that way."

My father told me, when I went to him crying with a broken heart, "It's just a phase you are going through."

I stand against the lie that I do not have the right to have my own feelings. I want to feel it all: the pain, the sorrow, the guilt, the angst, the grief, the joy, the ecstasy! I am alive, and I will feel all the feelings that go with being alive.

PRAY

Lord, I want to feel the full range of feelings that you have given me. As I grow closer to you, I want to feel what you would feel about people and situations. I want to cry about the things that make you cry. I want to rejoice about the things that make you rejoice.

TAKE ACTION—MARRIED OR SINGLE MAN

You may have trouble identifying your feelings other than the most basic ones like joy and anger. Make a conscious effort to identify your feelings during the day as you deal with various situations.

Journal about the feelings you are experiencing. Consider that you may be stuffing feelings due to childhood issues. Added to that is the fact that porn numbs your feelings.

What are you feeling right now? Identify each feeling in one word. To help you identify your feelings, check the *Feeling Words* chart in the Appendix.

Day 23

SQUARE ONE

*And let us not grow weary of doing good, for in due
season we will reap, if we do not give up.*

GALATIANS 6:9

My recovery has included times when I relapsed into sexual sin. It was discouraging. Even though I learned much and progressed far, when I sinned again, I felt as if I were back at square one.

But was I really back at square one?

No, I wasn't.

Was I wrong? Yes. But I repented. I turned back to the Lord. And I continued on in His power.

If I would make a graph of my recovery, it would show that I am on the right trajectory. I am headed toward total sexual purity the way the Lord intended it to be so I was definitely not back at square one. I am in the process of being sanctified, and my mind is being renewed every day.

I will not be discouraged or give up because with the Lord's strength and grace, I will have victory.

I see my future as living in purity and no longer struggling. With Him all things are possible.

PRAY

Lord, I get discouraged when I fall. Give me a sense of your
encouragement when this happens, and help me to dust
myself off and stand up again. I believe that all things are
possible with you. It is your will that I live a pure life, and
I desire to do your will. Thank you for caring about me.

TAKE ACTION—MARRIED OR SINGLE MAN

What practical safeguards can you put in place this week that will help you not to relapse?

_____

_____

_____

What was going on in your life the last time you relapsed?

_____

_____

_____

What were your feelings beforehand and afterward?

_____

_____

_____

How can you use this information to prevent future relapses?

_____

_____

_____

Check in with your accountability partner for support in this area.

Day 24

HONOR THEIR FEELINGS

*We ought always to give thanks to God for you, brothers, as
is right, because your faith is growing abundantly, and the
love of every one of you for one another is increasing.*

2 THESSALONIANS 1:3

I allow everyone around me to have and express their feelings, and I will not censor them. When people around me are able to express their feelings, it gives me an opportunity to better know them. They have a right to their own feelings, and I will honor that. It is okay to ask questions for more understanding.

I know how it is to have my feelings denied. Because of that, I will listen without judging whether I think they are justified or not. Their feelings are simply their feelings. Their feelings may be upsetting to me, but they are not mine to manage.

PRAY

Lord, I am so grateful for all you are teaching me as I go through the process of healing and getting back in touch with my feelings. Help me to allow other people to have their feelings and allow me to be comfortable with them. Our feelings may differ, but help me to allow you to work in them as you have worked in me.

TAKE ACTION—MARRIED OR SINGLE MAN

You will have to be deliberate about listening to others' feelings. Good listening takes practice. Make eye contact and sit on the edge of your chair if seated. Lean toward the person speaking. Show your engagement in the conversation by asking reflective questions, like, "So what I hear you saying is this, is that correct?" Overcome your urge to justify, criticize, or negate their feelings in any way. Do not argue about how others feel; they own their feelings. You may respond by saying, "Thank you for sharing your feelings about this. I really want to know how you feel about it." Acknowledging others' feelings is critical in your own healing process. It works to destroy the isolated and distorted reality we get from sexual addiction.

Day 25

HE'S POWERFUL ENOUGH

Seek the Lord and his strength; seek his presence continually!

1 CHRONICLES 16:11

On my own, I was not able to stop myself from falling into sexual sin. It's not that I hadn't tried over and over again—I did, but with no success. I was discouraged and ashamed and was getting to the point that I thought no one could help me break this addiction—not even God. I believed that if I went to God, He would be ashamed of me and not care to help me. But I was wrong.

God does care. He sent His Son to die for my sins—yes, even those sins. As I contemplate the strength of the Lord, I think about all the stars in the sky—how He created all the stars and galaxies in the universe, which are vast beyond my imagination.

He knows everything. God knows how many hairs are on your head. He loves every person and does not want anyone to perish. Yes, God is powerful enough to help you become sexually pure, and He loves you enough to want to help you through the process.

PRAY

I look to you, Lord, and to your strength to help
me arrive safely on the other side of this journey
to sexual integrity. I grow closer to you every day.
Thank you for loving me through the process.

TAKE ACTION—MARRIED OR SINGLE MAN

God is powerful enough to help you overcome your sexual sin. Trust Him.

When have you called on the Lord to demonstrate His strength in your life?

_____

_____

_____

_____

_____

_____

_____

_____

_____

How have you experienced God's power in your life? List five of the ways.

1. _____

2. _____

3. _____

4. _____

5. _____

Day 26

PURE AND FREE

*Out of my distress I called on the Lord; the
Lord answered me and set me free.*

PSALM 118:5

I tried for years—on my own power—to quit looking at porn. It didn't work! I was even hesitant to talk to a pastor or a friend because I thought I must be the only Christian who struggled with pornography.

Why did I think that? Because no one had ever confided in me with his porn problem. I never heard it brought up in a Bible study, a small group, or choir; so what was I to think? My logical conclusion? *You can't talk about a pornography problem at church.* After all, what would others say if they knew that I—a member of the choir and regular Sunday school attendee— was looking at porn and couldn't stop?

This is precisely where Satan wanted me to be: isolated and enslaved—but this is not what the Lord wants. I now understand that I can live pure and free in Christ. He died for this sin—and all my sins. This sin is not greater than every other sin in the world, and it is not uncommon—as I had once believed.

But how can I live pure? Christ wants me to rely on Him and His power instead of my own strength. I had to go to God humbly and ask for His help. It was the only way for me to be truly free.

PRAY

Lord, thank you for opening my eyes to the fact that,
with your resurrection power, I can do all things. *All
things* includes breaking the chains that porn has
had on me. Thank you for grace greater than my sin.
Thank you for your power to overcome my sin.

TAKE ACTION—MARRIED OR SINGLE MAN

It is comforting to know that we can do all things through Him who strengthens us. What does it mean to you to rely on God's strength?

Was it hard for you to humble yourself and confess to God that you needed help?

What was the turning point for you to be able to admit your weakness?

Day 27

DIRTY ROTTEN LIAR

When he (the Devil) lies, he speaks his native language,
for he is a liar and the father of lies.

JOHN 8:44, NIV

I have realized that Satan is the father of lies. He has told me lies about myself and lies about God. He has told me that sexual sin is not that bad. "Everyone else is doing it . . . You're not hurting anyone looking at porn . . . No one will ever know . . . Besides, you deserve it after a hard day at work." Lies. All lies.

Then after I gave into it he would say, "God won't want you now . . . You are no good . . . He no longer loves you . . . You're worthless." More lies.

And after all this, it even seemed as if Satan laughed at me. This is no friend. By the way, another lie of his is that there is a "party" going on in hell. Not true.

I am through listening to Satan's destructive lies. I am getting my information from God's Word. God loves me and cares for me. His guidance is for my good, and not to do harm or deprive me of fun. As the song says, "Trust and obey, for there's no other way, to be happy in Jesus, than to trust and obey."

PRAY

Lord, I have been fooled by the Devil's lies in the past. With your strength and grace, I can resist those lies. I am putting your Word in my heart so I will recognize the ways of the Evil One.

TAKE ACTION—MARRIED OR SINGLE MAN

What lies have you been told by the Devil about your sexuality? List them.

_____

_____

_____

_____

What verses can you memorize to have the Word in your heart to defend yourself? Make a list.

_____

_____

_____

_____

What are some of the realities about God's love for you? List them.

_____

_____

_____

_____

Day 28

GOD QUEST

Indeed, I count everything as loss because of the surpassing worth of knowing Christ Jesus my Lord. For his sake I have suffered the loss of all things and count them as rubbish, in order that I may gain Christ.

PHILIPPIANS 3:8

Lost in a darkened room at 2:30 a.m., the family asleep, I was about as far away from God as I could get. Not because I wanted to be, but because the shame and powerlessness I felt for giving in to evil made me feel so distant from God.

How did I get so far gone? How can I get control of my life again? Nothing I have tried to do on my own has worked for very long.

I would say to myself, *Now I will be dragging at work again because I am so tired. I'll be lucky if I don't lose my job because of this secret sin life.*

Finally, there arrived the day when I came to my senses and surrendered myself to God. I finally humbled myself and admitted to Him that I could not do this on my own—that I needed His help. I was willing to give up the sin even though I didn't know how I would ever be able to do it. This was the day I really started on my quest to know God more and deeper than ever before.

PRAY

Lord, I want to know you more. I want to bask
in your love. Help me to be faithful to follow
you. I take comfort in knowing the Holy Spirit
is in me to guide and strengthen me.

TAKE ACTION—MARRIED OR SINGLE MAN

If you haven't joined us in the battle yet, it is time to work on your purity. Don't put it off another day.

What are some things you can do to support your new efforts to know God more?

_____

_____

_____

_____

_____

_____

What are some of the verses you are memorizing?

_____

_____

_____

_____

_____

_____

Start with some of the verses in this book.

Day 29

LIVIN' FORGIVEN

*If we confess our sins, he is faithful and just to forgive us
our sins and to cleanse us from all unrighteousness.*

1 JOHN 1:9

In the dark days of addiction, I felt anything but forgiven. I was afraid of God. I was in hiding. The Bible said that I would be forgiven, but my sin was so bad and so dark that surely it could not be included under the forgiveness blanket. God is good, but I was pushing it way past the limits—my limits and His limits.

A problem with sexual sin is that it carries you farther than you want to go. Later, you want to go farther, but not as far as the porn takes you. Down and down you spiral until you feel as if you are at the bottom of a very deep, black, dank pit with steep sides and no way out.

I am so thankful for God's forgiveness and how it has pulled me out of the pit. The Lord understands what it is like down there, and He wants to help. I can now focus on the promises of the Bible, which were hidden from me in the pit.

I had believed the lie that God did not love me anymore and wouldn't forgive me. I have replaced that lie with the truth that I am loved and forgiven. It is a process, but I am learning to walk in that forgiveness one day at a time. I am forgiven.

PRAY

Lord, thank you for your vast love and your grace to
forgive me. Help me to live out my life as a forgiven person.
Help me not to slip back into feeling that I'm condemned.

TAKE ACTION—MARRIED OR SINGLE MAN

Reflect on a time when you felt you were in a deep, dark pit. Describe your rescue from that pit and how it has impacted your life.

From here on out, remember to stay far away from that pit. Don't ever think that you can stand at the edge and look down inside. Stay far away. If you are tempted to go there, run the opposite direction. Don't walk. Call your accountability partner and talk it through. Go meet with him for extra support.

Day 30

I WANT HEALING

When Jesus saw him lying there and knew that he had already been there a long time, he said to him, "Do you want to be healed?" The sick man answered him, "Sir, I have no one to put me into the pool when the water is stirred up, and while I am going another steps down before me." Jesus said to him, "Get up, take up your bed, and walk." And at once the man was healed, and he took up his bed and walked.

JOHN 5:6–9

It's interesting that the man at the pool did not say, "Yes, I want to be healed." Instead, he gave an explanation of why he wasn't healed yet, that he needed someone to help him. He had tried on his own but couldn't get to the healing waters in time.

Well, I needed help too, and I no longer hesitate in saying that I *do* want to be healed. I was so done with pornography dominating my life. I was sick of it. I was sick of doing what I didn't want to do, and sick of doing what God didn't want me to do. I tried on my own, but I couldn't overcome it. I am thankful that God can heal and that He is available to me when I seek Him. God has grace to cover this sin, and I can draw upon it.

In his classic *My Utmost for His Highest*, Oswald Chambers said, "Grace is the overflowing favor of God, and you can always count on it being available to draw upon as needed." I have called upon that grace; and I pray you will too—every time you need to.

PRAY

Lord, with your power I can be free of the chains
of sexual addiction, just as this man was healed
of his sickness. Thank you, Lord, for your grace
for me—a sinner—who will walk victoriously.

TAKE ACTION—MARRIED OR SINGLE MAN

You have to decide; do you want to be healed or not? You have to want it badly. The goal of just being better than you have been—or looking at porn only once in a while—is the wrong goal, and it won't work.

You can truly be free in Christ. Why settle for anything less? It is really up to you to make a commitment. Are you willing? God will be there for you when you are ready.

Write out your commitment now. Pour out your heart to the Lord. He loves you. He died for all your sins—all of them. Our God is a big, great, loving God.

Day 31

DIFFICULT, BUT WORTHWHILE

But Jesus looked at them and said, "With man this is impossible, but with God all things are possible."

MATTHEW 19:26

It takes courage to look yourself in the mirror and say, "I am a sex addict." But until you do, the addiction drags and only gets worse. You need bravery and courage to reach a pure life. It's a difficult path.

Anything worth doing will take work, but it is worth it! This journey is teaching me a lot about myself, improving many aspects of my life. It's not just about sex, but about how I deal with stress and where I turn for comfort.

Most importantly, my purity journey has helped me to put God first and rely on His strength. Without God it would be impossible. My faith is deepening as I clearly see God working in my life. As soon as I reached out to Him to help me with my purity, He was right there. My Lord, my wife, and my family are all rooting for my success.

PRAY

Lord, this is it. I am ready and willing to be healed.
I am willing to face the addiction and do whatever
it takes to be pure. I rely on your strength to
do what I could not do on my own.

TAKE ACTION—MARRIED OR SINGLE MAN

What have you faced in the past that seemed impossible, that you were able to do with God's help?

_____

_____

_____

_____

_____

Keeping a list of these will build your confidence—that you have faced difficulties in the past and can expect to conquer more in the future. God is faithful to see you through every difficulty, even the struggle for purity. Resolve now that you will do whatever it takes, with God's strength, to live a pure life.

List five impossible situations that you overcame with God's help.

1. _____

2. _____

3. _____

4. _____

5. _____

You can do it!

Day 32

NO MORE EXCUSES

*Repent, then, and turn to God, so that your sins may be wiped
out, that times of refreshing may come from the Lord.*

ACTS 3:19, NIV

Anger was one defense mechanism I used to cover up my sin and protect it. I felt as if everyone was a bother and should leave me alone.

"I'm alright."

"I can quit any time."

"I've quit many times before."

"Just get off my back!"

"I can handle this on my own."

"I'm not going to a counselor; maybe *you* should go to a counselor."

Sound familiar? This is how I talked before I sought help. Sexual sin's power over me has weakened because I'm not hiding it any more. I have ripped the veil off the sin, and it lies exposed for what it is. I have turned from my sin 180 degrees. I quit blaming my wife, my family, my job. It is—and was always—my own doing. I will no longer defend it.

PRAY

Lord, thank you for loving me through this process.
Please bring healing through my accountability partner.
Bring healing to my relationship with you and the people
in my life. I know I can succeed only in the resurrection
power of Christ. Thank you for grace to face this issue.

TAKE ACTION—MARRIED OR SINGLE MAN

In most cases, the root source driving sexual sin is pain and disappointments from the past. It may stem from early childhood when adults created a chaotic atmosphere. It can result from pain and heartbreak in adult life: a broken relationship, job loss, or any number of sources.

List your pain and disappointment from the past, and ask God to bring healing to each one of these hurts. Consider what Jesus might have said if he were there with you physically in each painful situation.

Painful experiences you've had in life:

1. _____

2. _____

3. _____

4. _____

5. _____

What would Jesus have said to you in those situations?

1. _____

2. _____

3. _____

4. _____

5. _____

Day 33

HIGHER-PURPOSE DRIVEN

But seek first the kingdom of God and his righteousness,
and all these things will be added to you.

MATTHEW 6:33

In the depths of my addiction, my only thought was about my own comfort and no one else's. I was pushing God way down on my priority list. Even when I spent time with my family, our activities were overshadowed by my thinking about when I could look at porn again. Lusting after women had become a hobby that was all about placing my pleasures over everything and everyone else.

When my purpose was only to serve my own comfort and convenience, then I acted in a sinful way, doing whatever felt good at any given moment. I was always seeking after being happy and having fun. If this is where you are—or where you've been—I get the mindset, *Well, I can look at porn because I had a hard day, and I deserve it.*

When I was in that frame of mind, I was just serving my own pleasures and not the pleasures of God. I was easily drawn into sexual sins, drinking too much, and devoting too much time to leisure of all sorts. The problem was this: whatever I did, or whatever I had, it didn't satisfy. It was never enough. It couldn't be enough because it wasn't of God. As Solomon's words tell us, without God, "Everything is meaningless" (Ecclesiastes 1:2, NIV).

As I began healing and spending more time studying the Bible, I learned that my purpose here on earth is a much higher purpose than serving myself. I learned that I am called to serve God. As I live out my life serving God, I am becoming more satisfied with my life.

PRAY

Lord, help me focus on my purpose of serving you. With this right focus, the things of comfort will have less of a pull on my life. It will be easier to stay pure. Thank you for giving my life a higher purpose.

TAKE ACTION—MARRIED OR SINGLE MAN

What did you chase after for your own comfort and convenience? Make a list of at least five things.

1. _____

2. _____

3. _____

4. _____

5. _____

Are you still holding on to some things? If so, what are they? Make a resolution to live for Christ and not yourself.

_____

_____

Write about how your life is changing while you are on your purity journey. List the changes you have seen.

_____

_____

_____

Day 34

RADICAL SURGERY

*And if your hand or your foot causes you to sin, cut it off and
throw it away. It is better for you to enter life crippled or lame than
with two hands or two feet to be thrown into the eternal fire.*

MATTHEW 18:8

Sin is serious, and I have taken radical measures against it. I needed to cut sexual sin out of my life, just as a surgeon removes a malignant tumor. And still, I must be on my guard to be proactive in my fight for purity—but not in my own power. I've tried it by myself. It didn't work, which is why I finally sought help. Now I have the guidance of the Holy Spirit, the outrageous grace of God, and the resurrection power of Christ for the strength I need.

With all of that support, I call my accountability partner during the week and memorize Bible verses. I have even added accountability software on my computer. I also protect my children by keeping parental controls in place and talking openly about the use of technology and its hazards.

My computer use is now limited to my work. Even better, I have adjusted my computer monitor to face the door of my office. Our home computer sits in the living room so everyone in the room can see the screen. I will continue to be diligent and proactive and take every step to guard my purity and that of my family.

PRAY

Lord, thank you for loving me through this healing
process and being right there for me to rely on your
power. I am serious about wanting healing, and I put
all my faith and trust in you. I know that sin is serious
and that sexual sin is particularly destructive to me. I rely
on you because on my own, I cannot overcome it.

TAKE ACTION—MARRIED OR SINGLE MAN

How badly do you want to get pure? Are you willing to take radical action steps—and step out of your comfort zone? To win this battle, that's exactly what you'll need. You will really need to have your priorities right and count on your accountability partner. With much prayer, the guidance and power of the Holy Spirit, and good accountability, you can do it.

Why would the Bible tell about a radical approach to sin like cutting off a hand or a foot? Write down your answer.

_____

_____

_____

_____

_____

What are some radical, surgery-like things you can do to fight your sexual addiction? Which steps will you take right now? List them.

1. _____

2. _____

3. _____

4. _____

5. _____

Day 35

EVERY THOUGHT CAPTIVE

We take captive every thought to make it obedient to Christ.

2 CORINTHIANS 10:5, NIV

For years my mind was cluttered with thoughts of sexual lust. My thoughts were almost constantly focused on something to do with lusting after women. It was difficult to concentrate on anything else.

However, I now am able to calmly take each one of those thoughts as it enters my mind and make it obedient to what Christ wants for healthy, godly sexuality in my life. As I continue to take those thoughts captive, my thinking is more Christlike; and fewer of those unwanted thoughts are entering my mind. This is a process, and you can expect to be very busy capturing these thoughts at first. I look forward to the future when my thought life will be more and more pure and manageable.

Even though I cannot control which thoughts enter my mind, I can take them captive to the obedience of Christ. The thoughts themselves are not sinful; it is what I choose to do with them that can become sinful.

PRAY

Lord, give me your strength to be more like you.
Give me the discipline to take each lustful thought
and turn it around so I see things with your eyes.

TAKE ACTION—MARRIED OR SINGLE MAN

Memorizing Scripture is a life changer for the sexually addicted. The verses deepen your spiritual conviction as well as work with your brain. Your brain needs the verses of truth to counteract the automatic responses of your limbic system and the lies you have been believing. The limbic system involves emotions, behaviors, and long-term memory.

Start by memorizing the verse in this devotion. List other verses you plan to memorize, starting with Job 31:1. "I made a covenant with my eyes not to look lustfully at a young woman" (NIV).

If you don't yet have an accountability partner, ask another man to be accountable with you for memorizing verses. List some potential accountability partners. Start contacting them today.

Day 36

CLOSER TO HIM

*Since we have these promises beloved, let us cleanse
ourselves from every defilement of body and spirit,
bringing holiness to completion in the fear of God.*

2 CORINTHIANS 7:1

I was so buried and shamed in my sin that I was hiding from God. I was moving farther from Him, but at the same time, I was desperately worried that He would just abandon me. I didn't think He could ever forgive me for the terrible things I had done. My sin created distance between God and me that I didn't want. I yearned to be closer to Him.

Now, since turning from sexual sin and seeking Him, I am learning to accept the grace that is bigger than my sin. Now, it is still hard to wrap my mind around this, but I believe it by faith. I honor the Lord and want to do what He wants me to do. I continue changing direction and moving away from my sexual sins hour by hour, day by day.

Each day, I feel closer to God as I choose to be pure. I am so grateful that God loved me even when I was deep in my sin. I rejoice in the victory I have experienced so far, and look forward to more days of triumph as I get even closer to Him.

PRAY

Lord, thank you for your grace. Thank you for
loving me even when I am so unlovable. Your grace
is beyond comprehension. Help me to recognize
everything that contaminates body and spirit so I
can change and show my reverence for you.

TAKE ACTION—MARRIED OR SINGLE MAN

Do a 180-degree turn from your sins. Don't settle for 20 degrees or 100 degrees. Not even 179 degrees. It won't work. But remember—the only way that you will be able to turn 180 degrees is with God's help. Ask Him for His help right now.

If you are a Christ follower, you have the Holy Spirit dwelling in you. He wants you to rely on His power and not your own. He wants you to ask for His help, and He is right there . . . waiting. I have seen this happen in groups so many times with men who were trying to get pure on their own and finally surrendered the struggle to God. He was right there for them every time. Jesus is alive! The Holy Spirit is in you to guide you and strengthen you.

What can you do today to get closer to God? Make a list.

_____

_____

_____

_____

What is the next step for you to move away from your sexual sin? Write it down.

_____

_____

_____

_____

Day 37

THE END OF MYSELF

For my yoke is easy, and my burden is light.

MATTHEW 11:30

When I am honest with myself, I can admit that the burden of the sin was heavy and dark. What supposedly seemed fun—out drinking and carousing in the bars—only led to hangovers, lost Sundays, and a trail of broken relationships with women.

God warned me against this kind of "fun." Was it really the fun I thought it would be? I finally realized that I was leaving a trail of hurt people, wasted time, and squandered money. Abusing my body with alcohol and sex no longer seemed fun. It was leading to depression and a spiritual void.

I avoided facing my addictions for a long time, but finally I had to do something. My life was a mess. I was living a double life—one man at church and a different man everywhere else. Finally, I had come to the end of myself. I admitted that my way was not the better way, and that I had nothing of worth to present to my God. I needed Him.

I can now accept and enjoy the yoke that Jesus has for me. His yoke is easy when I quit trying to pull away and do things my own way. His yoke is not meant to harm me, but to help me. My burden is light. I now walk in the light, free by the grace of God.

PRAY

Lord, thank you for opening my eyes and for caring
for me with your love. I accept your yoke and am
happy for it. Your ways are higher than my ways.

TAKE ACTION—MARRIED OR SINGLE MAN

List five ways your eyes have been opened to the joys of His yoke.

1. _____

2. _____

3. _____

4. _____

5. _____

Recount to your accountability partner your own story of coming to the end of yourself. Write it down as a testimony to God's power demonstrated in your life.

_____

_____

_____

_____

Make a list of men with whom to share your testimony. It will give them hope.

_____

_____

_____

_____

_____

Day 38

PURE ALONE TIME

So teach us to number our days that we may get a heart of wisdom.

PSALM 90:12

Time alone in the house can be a dangerous time for my purity. Often in the past, I spent this time in sexual fantasy.

I will no longer look at my time alone in the house as a lawless sexual time. I view it in an entirely new way. When my family is not at home, I will do some healthy activities. I'll clean up around the house, work on a hobby, catch up on the bills, mow the lawn, or work on other chores.

That precious time alone is perfect for reading my Bible or preparing for my men's Bible study. By using my time wisely reading the Word, I will gain wisdom. I'll not waste the time or sexualize it.

PRAY

Teach me to use my limited time on earth
wisely. Help me not to waste it or use it for
sin, but to build up my household. Lord,
help me to keep my eyes upon you and
to enjoy time alone as an opportunity to
be with you. My hope is in you, Lord.

TAKE ACTION—MARRIED MAN

If you know you will be alone in the house sometime this weekend, what are things you can plan on doing with that time? Make a list now so you can go right to that list and get started when everyone else leaves. The focus will help you to stay out of trouble and be more productive. Have you ever complained that you have no quiet time to study the Bible? Well, here it is. Don't miss it.

Take up your favorite hobbies again. If you have no hobbies, is there one you've always wanted to start? Begin planning for a new hobby today! The next time you are alone in the house, you can work on that hobby or go to the store to buy the equipment you'll need. Include your accountability partner for some fellowship time.

SINGLE MAN

Being alone in your house is something you deal with every day. Create a plan for spending time at home. Consider starting a new hobby as suggested to the married men. Try hobbies that take you outside your home and involve other people. How about racquetball or golf? If you like reading, find a coffee shop and leave your computer at home.

Day 39

CONTROLLING MY TONGUE

Let there be no filthiness nor foolish talk nor crude joking, which are out of place, but instead let there be thanksgiving.

EPHESIANS 5:4

My tongue was a wild beast. I was quick and unapologetic with my cutting remarks. Lacing my speech with sarcasm, I used foul language at home more often than anywhere else—a throwback to what I had learned from my dad.

In discussing the topic of the tongue with Jim, one of my small-group leaders, he explained one source behind losing control of his tongue. Jim had long believed that he didn't deserve his lot in life. He thought he was entitled to better. This wrong attitude left him with a gnawing sense of dissatisfaction. He allowed himself to become frustrated with small nuisances, which made him feel grumpy. That grumpiness was his excuse for unleashing his tongue.

Listening to Jim's story made me realize the importance of self-control, and I began to discipline my tongue to speak in a way that brings glory to the Lord. There is no room in my life for negative speech. Silence is better than speaking in a nasty or degrading manner. Foul language is a sign that I could be heading toward a relapse into sexual sin. And I won't go there.

PRAY

Lord, fill my heart with you so my speech is an overflowing of your love, bringing glory and honor to you. Help me to control my tongue.

TAKE ACTION—MARRIED OR SINGLE MAN

To uncover patterns occurring when you lose control of your tongue, begin tracking these incidents in your journal or calendar. Include the context of each situation.

List measures you can take to prevent negative speech during your day.

Day 40

TERMINATE PROCRASTINATION

Therefore do not be anxious about tomorrow, for tomorrow will be anxious for itself. Sufficient for the day is its own trouble.

MATTHEW 6:34

Procrastinating used to be a way for me to create some of the tension of the crisis environment of my childhood. I have purposely waited until my car tabs were overdue by a week before purchasing them. I have put off doing my taxes so that I would be up half the night, driving downtown to mail them at midnight on April fifteenth.

Creating this pressure and tension supported my cravings for sexual sin, which is how I released the tension. Procrastination was a sick way for me to duplicate the chaos of my childhood, where the addiction was rooted.

Now that, with God's help, I have escaped procrastinating as a lifestyle, life is much smoother. I no longer wait to take care of things until the last minute—or later. My life is no longer filled with chaos and crisis. This newfound calm helps me to maintain my purity and my peace of mind. I may have been born into a chaotic home, but I do not have to live that way as an adult. I have a choice.

PRAY

Lord, help me to enjoy a peaceful life in you, not creating unnecessary pressure and tension. I give you all the glory for the purity I have experienced so far; help me to stay pure all my life.

TAKE ACTION—MARRIED OR SINGLE MAN

List all your activities in a typical week. Is there more than a reasonable number? If so, what can you remove from your schedule?

_____

_____

_____

_____

Write out how you take care of the necessary chores in your life. For example, groceries, housecleaning, car maintenance, doctor checkups, furnace maintenance, and the like.

_____

_____

_____

_____

Do you have a system or a schedule? If so, how is it working for you? If you don't, draft out a basic plan to get started.

_____

_____

_____

_____

Day 41

THE BROKENHEARTED

The Lord is near to the brokenhearted and saves the crushed in spirit.

PSALM 34:18

I recall the song, "What Becomes of the Brokenhearted?" from my teenage years. The lyrics resonated with me, but I wasn't sure why at the time. Just the title brings me to tears, even now. The song tells about being alone, searching for a caring person in your life—and having a sense of hopelessness.

While you may associate a broken heart only with romantic love, I think it can have other sources. Brokenheartedness from a difficult childhood is often part of what influences men to choose sexual sin. Unmet emotional needs lead to a broken heart.

Coming from a family with serious dysfunctions left me short on emotional care. It is the source of the brokenhearted, melancholy feelings.

Sometimes I have felt as if I am not as good as the other guys because I have struggled not to look at porn, even though I love God. But when I read God's Word, I see so many examples of how God has used brokenhearted people to further His kingdom. Here are two examples.

- God used David to slay Goliath, even when his father regarded him as incapable of being king—and then God used him to lead a nation.
- God took Joseph, whose brothers had sold him into slavery, and made him a great leader.

The stories of David and Joseph give me comfort. While I may be different from other guys, I am loved and can be used by God for great things. God will take what Satan meant for harm and use it for good, just as Joseph eventually explained to his brothers.

My past heartbreak gives me empathy for others who are facing their own broken hearts. I am so happy to know that God is close to the brokenhearted.

PRAY

Thank you for caring enough to rescue me, Lord.
I am one whose spirit was crushed. Thank you for
being close to me and all the brokenhearted.

TAKE ACTION—MARRIED OR SINGLE MAN

In examining life in your childhood home, work at uncovering sources of emotional pain that you may have taken for granted. It is not uncommon for some to think that abusive behavior is the normal way to live. Uncovering the truth about these things can be a painful process, but it is worth it.

Here is a humorous example. My brother-in-law had eleven children who grew up in a small house. When the children became adults and owned their own homes, they were amazed by how long their water heaters lasted. In the house with eleven children, they had replaced the water heater every year! The children grew up thinking that annual water heater replacement was normal.

What are some of the things that went on in your childhood that you thought were normal—but now you know otherwise? List them.

Day 42

GOOD COUNSEL

Plans are established by counsel; by wise guidance wage war.
PROVERBS 20:18

When I don't know what to do in a difficult situation with my wife or children, I will not fear, worry, or freeze as my dad did. He was not a healthy role model. While he did the best he could, he was not able to give me all the emotional support I needed. His judgment was often clouded by alcohol.

We all need emotional support, and there is good counsel to be found among my Christian brothers. The Word of God guides me. I am no longer afraid to admit that I sometimes do not have a clue about what needs to be done in a specific situation.

When I feel this uncertainty, I do not isolate myself and behave in a self-destructive way as I used to; but I now take action and ask for help and stay present. It is okay not to always have the answer.

PRAY

Lord, when I am unsure of what to do as a
husband or a father, help me not to panic or
worry, but to turn to you in prayer. I know that
you love me and want the best for me. I thank
you right now for all you have done in my life.

TAKE ACTION—MARRIED MAN

What steps can you take to get more support in your role as a husband, and as a parent if you are a father? List them.

_____

_____

Is there a group at church you can join? Sign up for it—or start it—today. Alternatively, seek out a man to be your mentor.

SINGLE MAN

As a single man, perhaps from a dysfunctional home, you too may find yourself wondering what to do in certain situations. Which situations make you uncomfortable? List them.

_____

_____

_____

You will need support in your role as a single man. Arm yourself with a dependable accountability partner and stay—or get—connected to other single men at church. Plan events together to grow your bond. Make a list of possible events.

_____

_____

If you don't know something, or don't have the answer, ask until you do. In prayer, ask for wisdom too, as it says in James 1:5. "If any of you lacks wisdom, you should ask God, who gives generously to all without finding fault, and it will be given to you" (NIV).

Day 43

RESOLVING CONFLICT

*Fear not, for I am with you; be not dismayed, for I am
your God; I will strengthen you, I will help you, I will
uphold you with my righteous right hand.*

ISAIAH 41:10

It is no longer appropriate to avoid conflict to protect myself as I did when I was a child. When my parents fought, I felt helpless and was unable to do anything about it. Back then I was powerless. Even though I did not grow up with a role model to demonstrate healthy conflict resolution, I am determined to break the cycle of dysfunction.

As an adult, I have found strength to resolve conflict in a healthy way. I am learning to deal with issues and face them as they happen. I enjoy a new sense of peace from facing whatever comes my way each day. I keep my life in day-tight containers, no longer carrying yesterday's conflicts into my today.

PRAY

Lord, help me to not shy away from
conflict, but to face each problem and
resolve it. With you I can do anything,
facing everything that comes my way.

TAKE ACTION—MARRIED OR SINGLE MAN

Make a list for each of the following questions.

What kinds of conflict do you fear?

_____

_____

_____

_____

What are some issues you commonly need to face?

_____

_____

_____

_____

Which ones are the most difficult for you and why?

_____

_____

_____

_____

Resolve to face the conflicts of life.

Day 44

CHILDHOOD TRAUMA

When I was a child, I spoke like a child, I thought like a child, I reasoned like a child. When I became a man, I gave up childish ways.

1 CORINTHIANS 13:11

I am exploring my childhood to determine what went on that created trauma and pain—things that caused emotional scars. I look back at my family knowing that no parents are perfect at raising children. I learned that from raising my own children.

My parents did the best they could at the time. I was the best kid I could be. I understand that the things that went wrong in my childhood household were not my fault. I am not looking back to find an excuse for my behavior or to blame someone else for my current situation so I can go on sinning.

What I am trying to do is find out who I am. Much has been glossed over, glazed over, and paved over. *Why am I where I am today? Where do I need healing? Did being rejected by the Little League really scar me with a message that I was not good at sports? Is that why I never tried out for any teams in high school?*

I recalled this Little League incident just recently and considered the possible effect it had had on me. Looking back, I understand why they didn't choose me. Being a left-hander, I had not developed the ability to catch with my right hand. I would catch with my left hand, take the glove off and throw with my left hand.

What traumatic things have inserted lies into my mind that need replacing with the Word of God?

In my future, I see a day when I understand myself much better. I will understand the underlying drivers of my past addiction and will have experienced healing. With the lies being replaced by the truths of God, I can move smoothly through life, avoiding the things that tripped me up in the past.

My future will be much happier and more pure. First, I need to find out who I am.

PRAY

Help me, Lord, to uncover the problems that cause ongoing pain, which I have been medicating with sexual sin. Bring healing, and help me now to act in a healthy, adult manner—giving up my childish reactions.

TAKE ACTION—MARRIED OR SINGLE MAN

Is there a lie steering your life in the wrong direction?

_____

_____

The scars are different for everyone. The source of your scar may seem minor to someone else, but what is of concern is the affect it had on you. For example, it could have been that your dad did not show up for the big football game, and you concluded that fathers were unreliable. You may have vowed, "I'll never trust Dad again." That also could have affected your relationship with your heavenly Father.

What are some of the vows you made as a child or as a young adult that do not work for you now? What is it that you are medicating with sexual sin?

_____

_____

_____

In your journal, list the ten worst things that ever happened to you. I know it hurts. As you get down the list, you will start to get into the possible traumas that have placed lies in your brain. What are the truths of God that can replace these lies?

Day 45

SELF CARE

Behold, what I have seen to be good and fitting is to eat and drink and find enjoyment in all the toil with which one toils under the sun the few days of his life that God has given him, for this is his lot.

ECCLESIASTES 5:18

I learned little about nurturing during my childhood. Sure, I had food, clothing, and a place to live, but other things were missing. My father was not emotionally available because of his own difficult upbringing, battle fatigue from fighting in World War II, and the cloud of alcohol that came with his constant drinking. My mother's upbringing was also reflected in her mothering style, which was not the warm-and-fuzzy mom of fairy tales. I learned just to try to take care of any nurturing on my own. This is also when I learned to substitute sexual things for missing nurturing.

As an adult, I am now experiencing the great love my Father in heaven has for me, a sense that I am lovable. I can relax sometimes and practice some healthy self care. I can take a vacation. I can go on a retreat, and I can spend time enjoying a concert or a show with friends.

I can even sit and read a book. Yes! This was unheard of in my childhood. I was always expected to be *doing* something, and reading a book was *not* considered *doing* something. I will allow myself the nurturing I missed as a child.

PRAY

Lord, I was not nurtured well as a child. Help me in this area. Teach me to nurture myself and to bask in your vast love for me.

TAKE ACTION—MARRIED OR SINGLE MAN

You may have placed yourself as the last priority in your life. Take time to do some self care for better physical, mental, and spiritual health.

Make a list of self-nurturing activities. Include some of these nurturing experiences in your schedule for this coming week.

Day 46

SHARING BURDENS

Carry each other's burdens, and in this way you will fulfill the law of Christ.
GALATIANS 6:2, NIV

In my childhood, asking for help did not bring positive results. I learned at a young age that if I wanted something, I would just have to get it for myself. In the same way, the dysfunction I experienced in childhood made it difficult for me to learn how to solve problems. My mom's advice on girls was, "All's fair in love and war." It was not helpful in resolving my girl issues.

Over time I am learning to ask for help from supportive adults in my life when I face burdens. I'm great at sharing other people's burdens, but have not done as well at letting others share mine. Expecting that I can do everything on my own is not realistic, and I'm getting better at asking for help.

If I need legal help, I seek out an attorney. If I need medical help, I go to the doctor. If I need help about personal or spiritual issues, I go to a Christian brother. The same is true if I am dealing with sexual issues. I can go to my wife and my accountability partner, and they will share the burden.

PRAY

Lord, I want to carry others' burdens and
let them fulfill the law by carrying my
burdens as well. It is still a foreign concept
to me—so Lord, help me to live it out.

TAKE ACTION—MARRIED OR SINGLE MAN

Make a list of people whom you can call on when you need help.

_____

_____

_____

_____

_____

_____

_____

_____

_____

_____

_____

_____

_____

Contact one of them to chat, and make an appointment to get together to develop your relationship.

Day 47

OUT OF ISOLATION

Do not be anxious about anything, but in everything by prayer and supplication with thanksgiving let your requests be made known to God.

PHILIPPIANS 4:6

I am leaving isolation behind to rejoin the rest of the world. As a child in my dysfunctional family, it made sense to isolate from the craziness of my parents so I shielded myself emotionally. The yelling at the dinner table frightened my sister and me. Oftentimes my sister would burst out crying and retreat to her room without finishing her supper. Withdrawing from this chaos seemed like a good idea when I was a child.

In adulthood, this kind of detachment no longer makes sense. It has affected both my reactions to difficulties, and my relationships with God and others. It has been a lot of work to change the isolation habit.

However, when something goes wrong now, I can better face it and deal with it confidently instead of isolating myself. I work to face difficulties and cope with life, solving problems one after another as they come. *Bring 'em on!* I am not afraid.

Isolation has also affected my relationships, but I'm building better connections with friends and neighbors and old church friends, selectively building a godly set of friends. These friendships had gone cold in my isolation, yet I am determined to rekindle positive relationships. As I emerge from my isolation, I am happy about a new, connected life. We're not meant to live this life alone.

PRAY

I ask for your strength, Lord, to face the problems that I have run away from in the past. Your Word says "Do not be anxious about anything." Help me be bold and face conflict with the confidence that comes with knowing you and trusting in your Word. Help me to rekindle healthy male friendships and make new friends as well.

TAKE ACTION—MARRIED OR SINGLE MAN

Isolating yourself is not appropriate or healthy. What are some specific steps you will take to emerge from isolation in a godly way, without sexual sin? List at least five of them.

1. _____
2. _____
3. _____
4. _____
5. _____

Is there a friendship lost due to your isolation that would be a positive one to rekindle? How about arranging a coffee or lunch appointment with that person? Call him today.

_____

_____

_____

_____

_____

_____

_____

_____

_____

Day 48

TRUE INTIMACY

Flee the evil desires of youth and pursue righteousness, faith, love and peace, along with those who call on the Lord out of a pure heart.
2 TIMOTHY 2:22, NIV

There was a time when sex was the most important thing in my life. It was the beginning and the end. All day long, sex was on my mind. It was either fantasy or lusting after passing women. A date night was expected to end with sex. Sex was the number one thing.

Of course, sex still has a place in my life, but now it is the way God intended it to be and not the distorted thing the world portrays. Sex is now the outcome of true intimacy with my wife, instead of the selfish pleasure of pornography. The world equates sex with lust; but God intended sex only for marriage. My life's new purpose is serving God instead of myself. He—not sex—is the beginning and the end.

PRAY

Lord, you created sex, and your law is
perfect. It protects me from the corruption
of the world. Guide me to your pure way
of sex. With your strength, I can be pure.

TAKE ACTION—MARRIED OR SINGLE MAN

Write about how your view of sex is changing as you heal. This is an opportunity for you to learn what God's Word says about sex and to start relearning what the world has taught you.

Day 49

FUTURE JOY

Run from sexual sin! No other sin so clearly affects the body as this one does. For sexual immorality is a sin against your own body.
1 CORINTHIANS 6:18, NLT

I used to try to minimize the impact of my sexual sin. I told myself many lies. *It's not that bad. All the guys are doing this. Why not? It's not hurting anyone. This is my relaxing time, my "me" time.*

I was right about that last one. It was selfish, and it was also destructive—but I couldn't see it at the time. The truth is that pornography ate away at who I was as a man. It diminished my ability to love God and all those dear to me. It destroyed my view of women. It was destroying my marriage. Viewing pornography was cheating on my wife, and no different from sex with a prostitute. It was false intimacy. I took what was sacred to the marriage bed and perverted it.

When I resolved to deal with this sexual sin and seek freedom in Christ, I began to see marriage the way God intended it to be. As I seek Him more, I experience true joy in anticipation of total freedom.

Right now I stand against any remaining strongholds of sexual sin. I see myself living without shame—the same man at home as I am in church. I rejoice that I can live a new transparent life—instead of the old double life.

PRAY

Lord, help me to feel how you grieve over sin.
Help me to take my purity seriously, and to rely on
your resurrection power to achieve it. I know that
on my own I cannot be pure; but with your Holy
Spirit guiding me, I can do it all for your glory.

TAKE ACTION—MARRIED OR SINGLE MAN

Write out the cost of continuing to stay in your sexual sin. List five items.

1. _____
2. _____
3. _____
4. _____
5. _____

What will be the real costs if you don't work on this now? What will your life look like in five years if you continue with your sexual addiction?

_____

_____

_____

_____

_____

Now on the positive side, make a list of the benefits of living a pure life.

1. _____
2. _____
3. _____
4. _____
5. _____

Day 50

I ACCEPT MYSELF

I praise you, for I am fearfully and wonderfully made.
Wonderful are your works; my soul knows it very well.

PSALM 139:14

When my wife and I are watching regular TV—not any adult-rated movie or anything like that—sometimes I just have to tell her that I can't watch the program and have to leave the room. At first this made me sad. I thought, *Why can't I be normal like other guys and watch this?*

Now I am learning more about myself and accepting who I am. I am unique, and my understanding of myself helps me to stay pure. Like an alcoholic who is careful about being around alcohol, I have to be careful about being around sexual things.

I am no longer ignorant of who I am as a person, and I can now accept myself as being perfectly made by God. I can guard my purity by carefully selecting and planning what I will watch. Even with careful planning, there may be times I have to leave the room or look away, but I have accepted this fact as a part of living with sexual integrity.

PRAY

Thank you, Lord, for helping me to understand
my uniqueness and not to resent it. You didn't
make a mistake. I am perfectly made by you.
Thank you for teaching me how to walk in your
way. Your way is better than the world's way.

TAKE ACTION—MARRIED OR SINGLE MAN

It is good to know that you are wonderfully made.

How do you see yourself as different from other guys?

_____

_____

_____

_____

_____

_____

_____

_____

_____

What precautions do you need to take to stay pure? List at least five.

1. _____

2. _____

3. _____

4. _____

5. _____

Day 51

BREATHE!

Be still, and know that I am God. I will be exalted among the nations, I will be exalted in the earth.

PSALM 46:10

I find myself still at the office after my workday should have ended—and rushing out to catch the last train home. Rushing from office to home after a day filled with meetings, long phone calls, e-mails . . . my day is packed with activity. On the way home, I find myself working on the train too, checking one more e-mail and making the final phone call of the day. I have learned that these kinds of work habits are related to the chaos of growing up in a family where simply relaxing and being still were not taught.

Both of my parents had full-time jobs. Evenings were crazy-busy-stressful. It seemed there was no time to breathe! I learned an important lesson about breathing as a participant in Adult Children of Alcoholics. One leader pointed out that many of us from dysfunctional families take very shallow breaths. That made sense, since many of us also smoked heavily, which might have been the only time we would breathe deeply.

I had never done deep breathing before. I've learned that it can help me relax, and it helps get me through temptation by relaxing the limbic system in my brain. The limbic system controls automatic responses.

My journey to purity has involved examining how I have dealt with problems in the past and developing a healthier way to live. I am learning not to jam my schedule so full. I'm building into my day time for recreation, time to exercise—and just time to breathe. And be still.

PRAY

Lord, I am used to running so hard and not even
allowing time to read your Word or talk to you
in prayer. Help me to keep my life in balance
and leave room to live, breathe, and be still!

TAKE ACTION—MARRIED OR SINGLE MAN

Take a look at your schedule. Lay out a plan to start clearing your calendar down to a manageable size. Include relaxation and just time to be still. Include time for your family, exercise, church, Bible reading, and memorization—and other positive pursuits that have been squeezed out by sexual sin. Remember to schedule time with your accountability partner. It is helpful to have an appointment time on your calendar that works for both of you.

Day 52

BREAKTHROUGH WILL HAPPEN

For this is the will of God, your sanctification: that you abstain from sexual immorality; that each one of you know how to control his own body in holiness and honor, not in the passion of lust like the Gentiles who do not know God.

1 THESSALONIANS 4:3–5

Life was very dark. My sense of hopelessness overwhelmed me. I wasted hours in sexual sin. I wondered if it was possible to ever be free of it. I even wondered if it was worth trying to escape. *Will I just fail again?*

I felt God must have just forgotten about me; or worse—that He had given me over to my sin.

However, I realized it wasn't true that He had given me over, or I wouldn't want to change. With His help, I made a commitment to purity. I made that commitment totally on faith since I certainly didn't "feel" it yet. Sexual integrity is not something that happens instantly.

Breakthrough will happen. I am staying the course. And you can too. With God's help, you won't give up. You have to keep on, even when you don't sense that you are getting anywhere. The process is slow.

It is like a peony, patiently waiting out the long winter. It doesn't even look alive. The plant looks just like dead sticks poking out of the ground. But then something happens. A little green starts pushing through the cold ground, even before all the snow has melted. It's not much, but it's a sign of life. That little plant keeps at it, looking at first like asparagus. Bravely it pushes up, branches, and buds out. Finally, gorgeous blooms open up.

You will know when that breakthrough has come. It will look like a glorious peony. The peonies bloomed outside the coffee shop where I wrote this paragraph. I can still smell the scent wafting across the sidewalk. The petals, soft as baby skin and so fragrant. This is the change of heart that I pray for all who are caught in sexual sin—from hard as stone to soft and pure, full of love and peace.

A change like this has come for me with steady focus and reliance on the power of the risen Savior. The Holy Spirit living in me guides me, counsels me, and powers my change.

On my own, I could not do this. I know. I tried. But with God's power, I get through each hour of each day. I can bloom and be everything that God intended me to be. And so can you. Take it one step at a time with the Holy Spirit. Your breakthrough will happen.

PRAY

Lord, I want to be pure. I am relying on you like never before to help me do what I cannot do on my own. Thank you for loving me and caring about me. Thank you for sending your Holy Spirit to live in me and guide and direct me.

TAKE ACTION—MARRIED OR SINGLE MAN

Be sure to get the Word of God into your heart. Memorize verses to give your mind the right focus.

What was the thing that made you finally decide to get on a purity journey? What verse(s) are you clinging to during this journey? Mine is Philippians 1:6.

TRUTH VS. LIES

But I fear that somehow your pure and undivided devotion to Christ will be corrupted, just as Eve was deceived by the cunning ways of the serpent.
2 CORINTHIANS 11:3 NLT

I am learning God's truths each day and replacing the lies that I believed during traumas in my life.

One of those lies was that *working through lunch and after hours will guarantee employment*. I realized it wasn't true only after I was terminated. I have learned the truth that I should work as if I am working for the Lord. I put my best effort into the work for the glory of God and not men.

Fathers are not dependable is another lie I believed. My own experience with my dad was that he was a loving man who sang to me as I lay down to sleep at night; but he was also angry and offensive when he drank too much alcohol. I have learned the truth: Dad did the best he could . . . and I have a heavenly Father who loves me consistently and constantly.

I once believed the lie that *porn is just a hyper version of sex that is okay*. I have learned the truth that it is a sin against my own body and it destroys relationships—with God and people.

God has taught me the truth: that I have been adopted into His family, and that He is my dependable Father who loves me and protects me. I am experiencing God's love as He gives me the strength to conquer sexual addiction. He not only wants me to be a conqueror, but He also wants me to be *more* than a conqueror.

PRAY

Thank you, Lord, for your truth. Open my eyes as I uncover the lies I have believed, and replace them with the truth of your love for me. Help me to use your divine weapons to demolish strongholds in my life.

TAKE ACTION—MARRIED OR SINGLE MAN

There is a battle going on for your mind. God has the truth and wants you to believe it. Satan wants you to believe his lies.

Look at my examples about the workplace and my earthly father. What similar lies (not related to sex) have you believed? What is the truth you now know about them?

False Belief   *The Truth*

_____   _____

_____   _____

_____   _____

_____   _____

_____   _____

_____   _____

_____   _____

Day 54

I'VE BEAT IT!

Keep a cool head. Stay alert. The Devil is poised to pounce, and would like nothing better than to catch you napping. Keep your guard up. You're not the only ones plunged into these hard times. It's the same with Christians all over the world. So keep a firm grip on the faith. The suffering won't last forever. It won't be long before this generous God who has great plans for us in Christ—eternal and glorious plans they are!—will have you put together and on your feet for good. He gets the last word; yes, he does.

1 PETER 5:8–11, MSG

After a period of sexual purity, I felt as if I had this thing beat. Then one Saturday afternoon I went to a bookstore and found myself paging through romance novels. I stopped short, shocked at my own behavior. I really thought I had beat this thing—and that this wouldn't happen anymore. I panicked at first. Could I really get free of this? Realizing right then and there that it wouldn't be that easy, I committed myself to stick with the program. I was determined to succeed.

My sinful nature was alive and well, and it played tricks on me. I had to remain alert and vigilant. I realized that I did not have this thing beat. Entrenched habits take time to break—and stay broken. Those patterns, literally etched in my brain, would take time to be rerouted. There is no shortcut. Time is required. I decided to give myself the time necessary to be clean, and to stay alert. While it is great to experience moments of victory, be careful; one battle does not win the war.

I continue to examine my life to learn more about myself and why I turned to sexual sin to cope with life's problems. I still need more healing. Praise God that the Bible acknowledges this issue in 1 Peter 5:8.

PRAY

I thank you, Lord, for giving me a period of
victory over the sin. Help me to stay aware and
keep a firm grip on my faith in you. Without
you, I would have no reason to desire to be pure
and no way to resist the pull of pornography.
But you have overcome the world. Thank you
for loving me and showing me such grace.

TAKE ACTION—MARRIED OR SINGLE MAN

Don't be fooled by a false sense that you are cured after a month or two. Be very cautious. Even though it is nice to finally experience some victory, you can't let your guard down. The Devil is ready to pounce.

Come up with some new safeguards to make it easier for you to stay pure. List at least five. It's not about "white knuckling it." You have to plan for your success.

1. _____

2. _____

3. _____

4. _____

5. _____

Day 55

GOOD REST

*Husbands should love their wives as their own
bodies. He who loves his wife loves himself.*

EPHESIANS 5:28

On this healing journey, I need to communicate more with my wife. I have learned to go to bed when she goes to bed. This is a good time to talk, and I can express my love and concern for her. Talking together gives me a chance to listen closely to her concerns and needs. I will have an opportunity to show my love for her. I will also be able to talk about my dreams for our marriage.

As a couple, we need to reestablish true intimacy a little at a time. I cannot expect that a minor attempt at intimacy will lead to sex. I have to get that goal out of my mind. After true intimacy has time to develop, sex will be a natural outcome.

We will take time to pray together and pray for one another. I am only starting to realize the extent to which I have hurt my wife; and she needs my care and attention. Going to bed when she does keeps me away from electronic devices, which are hazardous to my purity. I will stay in bed too, instead of getting up in the middle of the night to look at TV or the computer or any other electronic devices.

PRAY

Lord, thank you for giving me a wonderful wife. Open
my eyes to see her in a new and wonderful way and
treasure her as the special gift that she is. Help me with the
discipline to go to bed early. Please bring healing to her
heart and help us to build true intimacy in our marriage.

TAKE ACTION—MARRIED MAN

Many men are viewing porn at night after their wives are asleep. Going to bed with her is a simple step you can take to help yourself win your purity battle. It has a lot of other benefits as well.

Make a schedule for your evening activities so that you can be ready to go to bed with your wife. If you consider yourself a night owl, you will have to make adjustments in order to help build intimacy with your wife. It is better to strengthen your marriage than to indulge in your night-owl tendencies.

SINGLE MAN

Many single men are staying up late watching porn. When making purity a priority in your life, you have to be disciplined about how you spend your time and the rest you get each night. If you are up until 3:00 a.m., you will be tired the next day. A tired man is a man vulnerable to sexual impurity.

Make a schedule for your evening activities so you can get to bed, by 10:00 p.m. if you have a regular day job. You will be rested and better able to face the challenges of the day.

Day 56

IT TAKES TIME

So humble yourselves before God. Resist the devil, and he will flee from you.
JAMES 4:7, NLT

Other men may break from sex addiction more—or less—quickly than you do. I encourage you to neither brag nor beat yourself up, but remain humble and teachable. Giving up is not an option. Working the program and staying in the Word are the cornerstones.

Put safeguards in place to aid yourself in experiencing freedom. Your daily duties will be to memorize and reflect on Bible passages, and to call your accountability partner. God's strength—not your own strength—will be your power source.

Put in maximum effort to read and listen to helpful recovery material to assist your understanding. Being proactive is required to win.

Fully surrendering to God is a process, and some men are able to surrender their will and their addiction to God sooner than others. Trust God that you can become free of sexual sin the way thousands of men have done. Your healing will take place in God's perfect timing.

PRAY

I know, Lord, that all things are possible with you. I also understand that your timing is not my timing. I put my recovery into your hands, relying on your strength and your timing in my life. You are the Lord of my life.

TAKE ACTION—MARRIED OR SINGLE MAN

Examine yourself. Are you "all in?" Are you a fully-devoted follower of Christ? If not, what seems to hold you back?

_____

_____

_____

Are you still trying to do this on your own? If so, what do you need to let go of?

_____

_____

_____

To ramp up your commitment to getting pure, one thing you can do is count the cost of continuing in your sin. Make a list. If you continue, you could lose your family or your job. You could get into legal trouble.

_____

_____

_____

Do you still have secrets you are not discussing with your accountability partner?

_____

_____

_____

Day 57

OPEN AND HONEST

*Love one another with brotherly affection. Outdo
one another in showing honor.*

ROMANS 12:10

I have made my accountability partner a life-long support man. We have developed an openness to discuss personal, sexual matters. He knows my sexual struggle story like no one else, and I've kept in touch with him on a regular basis.

This man plays a critical role in my purity and my quest to know God more and love Him more. He is insurance against me slipping back into isolation. As our relationship grows, we are growing in the Word and living life together. It is good to have a strong Christian man to share the joys, fears, trials, and victories of life.

There will be times when I need help. I will need to talk to someone who understands. With that in mind, I will nurture our relationship, understanding how necessary—how critical—it is. I know I can always open up honestly about where I am in life.

Honesty is vital for the health of our relationship and for its effectiveness in helping me stay pure. He is in the trenches with me, and he has my back. I know I cannot fight it alone.

PRAY

Help me, Lord, never to take this relationship
for granted. Let it grow deeper each week. Let
me continue to be completely open and honest,
whether I am having a good day or a bad day.

TAKE ACTION—MARRIED OR SINGLE MAN

In order to keep an honest dialogue going with your accountability partner, develop some questions you will answer each week. Make them personal to your own situation. Here are a few examples to get you started:

Have you spent time in the Bible this week?

Have you been doing your best work at home and at your job?

What purity challenge will you face this week?

How are you doing in your thought life?

Have you been taking care of yourself by eating right and exercising?

Have you lied to me on any of your answers?

Day 58

FADING IMAGES

*Do not be conformed to this world, but be transformed by the
renewal of your mind, that by testing you may discern what is
the will of God, what is good and acceptable and perfect.*

ROMANS 12:2

The images from pornography seared vile pictures into my head. These images initially made it difficult for me to stop looking at it. It was like having videos playing in my head, even when I was not watching them.

These images slowly faded after I stopped looking at porn. It took some time, but the way to healing was to completely stop putting these images into my head. Instead, I started memorizing God's Word. This is when I started experiencing the renewing of my mind, as Paul explains in Romans 12:2.

My mind is being renewed. The Word crowds out the bad images.

Find strength and perseverance with the help of the Holy Spirit. It is His will that you live a pure life.

PRAY

Lord, I trust you to get me through this difficult
time of transition. You have good plans for
me and want the best for me. Please keep
transforming me and renewing my mind. I love
you and want to follow your commands.

TAKE ACTION—MARRIED OR SINGLE MAN

Memorize the Word of God so you can bring those truths to mind as you go through the day.

Create new images in your mind to replace the sinful ones that are fading. For me, visiting the Yosemite and Grand Canyon National Parks created amazing images that I love to recall.

List five wonderful new images you want to have in your mind.

1. _____

2. _____

3. _____

4. _____

5. _____

Trust that your mind will be renewed. The damage you have done will take time to repair, but it will happen for you. Stop feeding the porn monster—and it will die.

Day 59

MAN CAVE

I have come into the world as light, so that whoever
believes in me may not remain in darkness.

JOHN 12:46

The man cave for me wasn't a garage filled with antique garage signs and neon clocks. Nor was it a cool room with a pool table, a pinball machine, and a juke box with bubbles rising up the sides. Those man caves are the kind for inviting your friends over to have some fun.

My man cave was the late-night version of the family room. By day it was a place of laughter and family games, but at night it was a dark place of evil games. I sat by myself, with the lights low and the shades drawn, the DVD player was spinning the latest X-rated movie. It was a place of shame and isolation.

I am through with that solitary confinement. I have come out of hiding and into the light to join with my brothers in the fight for purity. There is healing in community, and God is there with us, "for where two or three are gathered in my name, there am I among them" (Matthew 18:20).

Maybe I'll buy a neon clock and hang some antique signs and invite some guys over to hang out in my new and pure man cave garage.

PRAY

Lord, thank you for your wonderful light. Thank
you for caring about me and drawing me out of
the darkness and into the light of your love.

TAKE ACTION—MARRIED OR SINGLE MAN

Did you isolate yourself as you got deeper into sexual sin? If so, explain how.

What interests and hobbies have you shelved due to sexual addiction? List at least five interests to renew as you heal and become free.

1. _____

2. _____

3. _____

4. _____

5. _____

Make a plan for your new, healthy man cave—a space where you can invite godly friends.

_____

_____

_____

_____

_____

_____

_____

_____

Day 60

MORE IN STORE

*And I am sure of this, that he who began a good work in you
will bring it to completion at the day of Jesus Christ.*

PHILIPPIANS 1:6

During this journey, there have been times when I was so low and feeling so far away from God that I felt as if there was no way back. The descent happened gradually. At first porn seemed fun and exciting. Before I knew it, it took more porn to generate the same intensity I first had felt so easily. Because of that, I sought a greater number and variety of sexual images.

Finally I realized that I was about to be cooked like the proverbial frog in the pot of steadily heating water.

Even so, I stayed in that boiling pot until a friend invited me to *The Battle*, a Saturday morning outreach using drama, a live band, and testimonies from both men and women. The morning ended with a call to action. It was there that I finally made a commitment to plant my flag and take my addiction to the Lord for help—to surrender to Him who died for all my sins.

The Battle event was followed by weekly platoon meetings, where I clung to Philippians 1:6. I was finally willing to stop viewing porn, but I was helpless to do it on my own. I needed the resurrection power that raised Christ from the dead.

Through my platoon meetings, I recognized that God had done many wonderful things in my life—and He wasn't done with me yet. He's not done with you either. He has good things in mind for you and will help you get pure if you surrender.

PRAY

Lord, thank you for never giving up on me. Thank you for loving me through the process of breaking free from sexual sin. You have been so merciful and loving to me.

TAKE ACTION—MARRIED OR SINGLE MAN

Make an exhaustive list of the ways God has helped you and answered your prayers.

Use this list as the beginning of a journal about your path to purity. Journaling will help clarify your thoughts and feelings as you heal. Journaling uses a different part of your brain than thinking, which is helpful for your healing. Don't be scared by the term *journaling*. It simply means to write down your thoughts.

Write freely for about twenty minutes a day. Feel free to buy a fancy journal in a bookstore, but if you find it intimidating to write in it, buy inexpensive, spiral-bound notebooks. Wherever you write, just write. There is more information on journaling in the Appendix.

Day 61

GOD IS SUFFICIENT

For you are great and do wondrous things; you alone are God.

PSALM 86:10

When I began to think that I needed to have something, do something, buy something, look at porn, flirt with women at the office, or drink alcohol in order to cope with life—or to be happy—I was putting that thing or action above God . . . and making it my god.

My old pattern of thinking went like this: *If only I had that new car, I would really be happy. If only I had more money, I could go to Europe, so I have to have more money.*

With that mindset, I decided to take a second job, which took me away from my family all the time instead of just part of the time. I made an idol—a god—of having money. When I did this, I was saying through my actions that somehow God was not sufficient for me, that our God was not doing well enough as Jehovah-Jireh, my provider.

I am learning that God is sufficient for my every need. I choose Him to be my top priority. I can live without my former sins, but nothing is higher than God and His Word. He wants the best for me, and I can be confident of that fact. He loves me so much that He sent His Son to die that I might be saved.

PRAY

Lord, this world presents many things as more important than you. Help me to focus on your sufficiency. There is nothing—and no one—more important than you. You are the beginning and the end. Your Son died for my sins so I can be free. Your power is sufficient to overcome all the alluring things of this world. Their power over me is fading with each new day in your light. You are the Light of the World. Thank you for your grace.

TAKE ACTION—MARRIED OR SINGLE MAN

When you start to think that you cannot live without something, beware. It may be emerging as an idol in your life.

What are five things that you have made into idols in your life?

1. _____

2. _____

3. _____

4. _____

5. _____

Put God first in your life again.

Day 62

HOLY SPIRIT GUIDED

*But the Helper, the Holy Spirit, whom the Father will
send in my name, he will teach you all things and bring
to your remembrance all that I have said to you.*

JOHN 14:26

In the midst of the addiction, I could hardly face God. I was like Adam, trying to hide from God behind the bushes in the Garden of Eden. As if I could hide from God—right! I didn't have time for my family, my neighbors, or God. I was isolated and spending my time and energy feeding my obsession.

I was ashamed and dared not reflect on the fact that, as a believer, my body is the temple of the Holy Spirit. While I tried not to think about it, the Holy Spirit would never stop nudging me that what I was doing was wrong. I was always aware of His presence.

As I heal from sexual sin, the Holy Spirit has been helping me to stay strong in my resolve. Rather than hiding in fear, I can now embrace and appreciate the Holy Spirit's guidance.

PRAY

Lord, thank you for not giving up on me when I tried
to hide from you. Thank you for your love and care.
Help me to be sensitive to the Holy Spirit's guidance.

TAKE ACTION—MARRIED OR SINGLE MAN

It's strange that we think we can hide from God. Of course we can't. Think about how the Holy Spirit works in your life. How have you been aware of the Holy Spirit who lives in you?

_____

_____

_____

_____

_____

_____

_____

_____

List five ways the Holy Spirit has helped you in your purity journey so far.

1. _____

2. _____

3. _____

4. _____

5. _____

Day 63

GOD'S WILL

Even before he made the world, God loved us and chose us in Christ to be holy and without fault in his eyes.

EPHESIANS 1:4, NLT

It seemed like porn was really working out for me. Whenever I needed an escape or relief, I could go to my pornography and get a jolt of pleasurable brain chemicals to feel good again. I was still faithfully attending church, Bible studies, and choir practice. I had really compartmentalized everything, as guys are so skilled at doing.

The Bible was quite clear that lusting after women and looking at porn was not acceptable. It was also clear that my wife hated my porn habit. I did feel some guilt and shame, even though I was in denial about her feelings.

I finally decided to—at a minimum—explore facing my sin. My problem was growing, but would it be worth it to go through the trouble of changing? And would I even be able to change?

I didn't know the answer to these questions, but I had to try. And now I know. You need to take it one step, one day at a time. My God is more powerful than any addiction. The Holy Spirit will guide you and strengthen you. There will be a new day when you are free and living in God's will.

PRAY

Lord, you are all powerful. You made the heavens and the earth. Help me now to live in your will—obeying your command to be holy because you are holy—and running from sexual immorality.

TAKE ACTION—MARRIED OR SINGLE MAN

Have you spent time searching for God's will for your life? Being sexually pure is part of being in God's will. Put everything you've got into living a pure life. How will it feel to know you are living in God's will? Write a description of what that means for you.

Day 64

LIGHT OF GRACE

For a day in your courts is better than a thousand elsewhere. I would rather be a doorkeeper in the house of my God than dwell in the tents of wickedness.

PSALM 84:10

In realizing the evils of porn, I can see wickedness spiraling down and leading to misery and despair. I'm revolted that the porn makers take advantage of vulnerable women who are on drugs and desperate for money for their next high. Other young women are lied to about getting into serious movie careers if they first perform in porn flicks. Still others, slaves of sex traffickers, are forced into making pornographic movies.

The smiles on those women are fake. The abuse is very real. The more I viewed porn, the more I realized that I was contributing to a lawless, filthy business where people are treated as disposable and without human dignity.

I have turned away from this sinful life and the destruction it causes. I am stepping into the light of God's grace. I am on a quest to know God more, and I get closer to Him every day. Receiving God's grace and embracing His ways now brings joy. I never want to go back to those evil ways. Instead of chains, I have freedom in Christ.

PRAY

Lord, help me to keep my focus on the joy of being close to you and growing more and more like you every day. Thank you for loosening the chains that held me in wickedness. Thank you for giving me your grace and sending me the Holy Spirit.

TAKE ACTION—MARRIED OR SINGLE MAN

Take time to think about the goodness of God. Think about His grace that is greater than all your sins. Reflect on how close you came to total destruction. Make a list of the relationships in your life for which you are grateful.

Day 65

GOD'S LOVE ENDURES

For I am sure that neither death nor life, nor angels nor rulers,
nor things present nor things to come, nor powers, nor height
nor depth, nor anything else in all creation, will be able to
separate us from the love of God in Christ Jesus our Lord.

ROMANS 8:38–39

I have seen men—actually weeping and crying—who are so ashamed of their behavior they have a difficult time believing that God can possibly still love them. They believed they were just too sinful and unworthy of the love.

In the midst of my sin, I felt this way myself; it is a desperate feeling, thinking that God has just given up on you. But didn't Jesus himself say we need to forgive, not seven times but seventy times seven? *Let's see, that is 490. Could it be that I am here asking for forgiveness for the 491st time? Have I exceeded the limit?*

Fortunately, God's grace is outrageously big. It exceeds the level of the sin. Of course, this doesn't mean that we should go on sinning. It does mean that He still loves us and wants a relationship with us.

I wanted not just to change my behavior, but to experience the full blessing of sex in my marriage the way that God intended. I could not settle for anything less than God's best for my life. I was ready. I accepted the assurance that nothing can separate me from the love of God.

Your habits may be so entrenched that you sometimes fall back into sin. While this is discouraging, do not allow it to throw you into despair. Remember that God's love and grace are bigger than your sin. Continue in your efforts toward purity. Then look forward to the day when your mind has been renewed to the point that you can say, "I am walking in purity and taking every thought captive to obey Christ."

PRAY

Lord, thank you for your grace. Thank
you for loving me even when I was far
from you. I want to do your will and get
even closer to you. Help me to live in
the purity that you intended for me.

TAKE ACTION—MARRIED OR SINGLE MAN

Think about where you would be without the grace of God. He loves you,
and He will love you through your current struggle. List five ways you feel
grateful for God's love and how He has shown His love in the past.

1. _____

2. _____

3. _____

4. _____

5. _____

Day 66

SATISFACTION IN CHRIST

You make known to me the path of life; in your presence there is
fullness of joy; at your right hand are pleasures forevermore.

PSALM 16:11

If we seek to find satisfaction in the things of the world, we will never find it. It illustrates a truth that Christians should understand. Solomon had everything, and yet he said it was all vanity.

As I grow in my faith, I am learning that true satisfaction comes from being close to Christ. He wants the best for us. He's not out to keep us from having any fun—that's what the world says about the Christian life.

His yoke is easy. You want a hard life? Take the sin route. I've tried it. It's a hard yoke without mercy and without love.

PRAY

Lord, I want to be closer to you and to
find my satisfaction in you. Help me keep
the world's pleasures in perspective.

TAKE ACTION—MARRIED OR SINGLE MAN

There is no denying that the momentary pleasures of the world are a huge draw. We want what we want, and we want it now. It is a childish attitude, but it is encouraged by our society, and we so easily buy into it. Commercials tell us all day long that we need things when we really don't.

Take a moment to think about all the "stuff" you have. Are you trying to find satisfaction in your stuff? What could you do without?

_____

_____

_____

_____

_____

_____

Write about how you would feel if you lost it all. What do you really need to be happy?

_____

_____

_____

_____

_____

Day 67

PURE MOTIVES

He who loves purity of heart, and whose speech is
gracious, will have the king as his friend.

PROVERBS 22:11

For me, sexual addiction was not only looking at pornography. The addiction included obsessing over women and the conquest of having them sexually. I was a ladies' man. My fear of pursuing sexual purity was that somehow I would end up being a boring prude, of no interest to women. I thought purity would require a personality change that was just not my usual extroverted self.

Obviously, I forged ahead in spite of my fear, and I realized that I'm not going to be any less appealing because I am pure. Somehow the image that I would be a dull, boring wallflower was part of my rebellion against making the effort to be pure—just another excuse.

I am regaining my sexual integrity and can enjoy women's company—free from any questionable motives and impure thoughts about them. I am enjoying my newfound purity, and am still myself—but much improved.

Through God's strength I am making the transition to sexual integrity.

PRAY

Lord, thank you for showing me again that purity
is your will for me. Thank you for loving me
through the process of being sanctified more
and more every day. You are so good. Thank
you for loving me with an unending love.

TAKE ACTION—MARRIED OR SINGLE MAN

List five preconceived notions you have that are slowing your purity progress.

1. _____

2. _____

3. _____

4. _____

5. _____

Do you fear that sexual purity will keep you from having fun? List five ways your life has improved by your purity efforts.

1. _____

2. _____

3. _____

4. _____

5. _____

Day 68

ONLY ONE TRUTH

But be doers of the word, and not hearers only, deceiving yourselves.

JAMES 1:22

There was a time when I followed what the Bible says, but only the parts that worked for me. I was reluctant to give Him my sexual life. My thought was this: *I want more from sex than what is in the Bible. I want porn and R-rated movies, strip clubs, and lust.*

It's as if I thought I had a better idea than God's. Those "extras" are what the world thinks are okay. They are a false "truth" about sex, but not the one true truth.

There is only one truth—the truth of the Bible, the truth that Jesus taught. Society has as many "truths" as the hardware store has paint colors. But these are not truths. The truths of God do not change with the decades. Sometimes a man tells me his decisions are guided by his "moral compass." In reality, that moral compass is just moral relativism; and it's not truth.

I need something more reliable and dependable than relativism. I need the unchangeable, immovable Truth of God. "Jesus Christ is the same yesterday and today and forever" (Hebrews 13:8). There is only one way to God, through His Son Jesus. Jesus is the Truth. That's what I'm talking about.

Understanding that Jesus has the truth—is Truth—I want to live according to what He says. As James 1:22 tells me, I must not be just a hearer of the Word, but a doer of the Word.

I have surrendered my life to Him and am not holding anything back. It is all His. Following Christ is demanding, but it is fulfilling and leads to a clear conscience. I want to be closer to God, my wife, and my family. I want my heart to break over the things that break Jesus' heart.

PRAY

Lord, I want to walk with you and get to know
you more every day. Thank you for your love.
Thank you for the truth. Thank you for helping
me to see through the lies that I had believed from
the wounds of my past. I want to experience
the joys of living according to your will.

TAKE ACTION—MARRIED OR SINGLE MAN

List five of the lies that you believed from the wounds of your past. What are
the truths that you believe now?

Lies	*Truth*

Write in your journal some of the ways these truths have changed your life.

Day 69

TIME WELL SPENT

Be very careful then, how you live—not as unwise but as wise,
making the most of every opportunity, because the days are evil.
Therefore do not be foolish, but understand what the Lord's will is.

EPHESIANS 5:15–17, NIV

I have wasted many valuable hours viewing pornography, lustfully looking at women, and fantasizing. I am thankful that God never let me alone when I looked at porn. He was always reminding me that I was wasting time. That was a grim time in my life, knowing that God was watching, and yet continuing to sin. Thanks to the Lord for never giving up on me.

As I focus on serving God and doing what is pleasing to Him, I see my life changing. Now I spend time developing healthy relationships. I spend my valuable time in the Word of God. His will is for me to live a pure life the way He describes it in His Word.

I remain open to the work God would have me do to further His kingdom. I do not want to waste any more of my time. I don't want to waste the precious life God has given me, knowing my time here is limited.

PRAY

Lord, I am so sorry for the time I have wasted
in lust. I rely now on your strength and mercy
to change. Thank you for opening up my
eyes and giving me more time to follow and
obey you. Your ways are better than my ways.
Your yoke is easy and your burden is light.

TAKE ACTION—MARRIED OR SINGLE MAN

Our lives are short and our lives are for serving the Lord, not indulging in selfish pleasures. Schedule time on your calendar for Bible study. As you move away from your life of lust, list five ideas for good ways to spend your time.

1. _____

2. _____

3. _____

4. _____

5. _____

Day 70

TAKING RESPONSIBILITY

Finally, be strong in the Lord and in the strength of his might. Put on the whole armor of God, that you may be able to stand against the schemes of the devil.

EPHESIANS 6:10–11

I was worried about my reputation, and I didn't want to fail at this. Yes, I was trying to escape from sexual addiction, but I had not given it my full effort. More importantly, I was not truly including the Lord, but simply relying on my own half-hearted effort. It wasn't working.

I guess I thought it would be easier than this—kind of a plug-and-play . . . and you're cured.

I blamed others: my wife, society, media, anybody but me! Early in my purity journey, with my lackluster effort, it was no surprise that I kept right on looking at porn and lusting after women other than my wife. My accountability partner was starting to wonder—and it was getting embarrassing.

I knew I had to stop. Things had to change. I had to take responsibility for my purity—to make the effort. Purity is a battle, and it will not be handed to anyone like a gift-wrapped present. To win this battle, I needed to put on the full armor.

It'll take everything you've got to succeed. And you'll need Christ's resurrection power to overcome. And when you do . . . keep right on marching forward in purity.

PRAY

Lord, help me to commit fully to do whatever it takes to be in your will and get pure with your power. I call on your strength to go boldly and confidently toward a pure life—the life you want for me.

TAKE ACTION—MARRIED OR SINGLE MAN

Make a new habit of putting on the full armor of God every morning. This is a daily—even a minute-by-minute—battle. You are changing how you deal with pain. This is no small thing, so buckle up and take full responsibility for your purity.

Memorize the full armor verses in Ephesians 6:10–17. Start by writing those verses in your journal.

Day 71

REJECTING FALSE INTIMACY

Do not be deceived: God is not mocked, for whatever one sows, that will he also reap. For the one who sows to his own flesh will from the flesh reap corruption, but the one who sows to the Spirit will from the Spirit reap eternal life.

GALATIANS 6:7–8

I lived so long with the false intimacy of porn. A computer screen and a man—this is not intimacy. It's an abomination. False intimacy drew me farther and farther away from real intimacy with my God, my wife, and my family. Even though those around me saw the isolation developing, I was unaware of how distant I had become, pulling away emotionally.

I have come to my senses. Real intimacy—starting with God first and then my wife—is what I am working on. I am grateful for a God who loves me and has so much grace. I know that reestablishing intimacy with my wife, family, and friends will take time. I will persist.

PRAY

Thank you, Lord, for loving me and wanting intimacy with me. I want to know you more. I want to call out to you, "Abba, Father." With your power and my sincere effort, I will do everything to establish intimacy with my wife, family, and friends. You are love.

TAKE ACTION—MARRIED MAN

Put some time into studying what intimacy means. It is not just sexual. You can create intimacy with your wife by things as simple as cooking a meal, making the bed, or taking a walk together.

What does intimacy mean to you?

_____

What can you do to increase intimacy with your wife? List five ideas, and ask her for input.

1. _____

2. _____

3. _____

4. _____

5. _____

SINGLE MAN

Real intimacy starts with Christ. Christ wants that intimacy with you. He wants a relationship with you. If you ask Him, He will forgive all your sins. Psalm 3:3 says, "But you, O Lord, are a shield about me, my glory, and the lifter of my head." You can go to Him without shame. Lift up your head!

How can you develop greater intimacy with Christ? List at least five ideas.

1. _____

2. _____

3. _____

4. _____

5. _____

Day 72

ABSTINENCE

For your obedience is known to all, so that I rejoice over you, but I want you to be wise as to what is good and innocent as to what is evil.

ROMANS 16:19

Single men, this devotion is primarily for the married man, but it is equally important for you to forgo any sexual activity for the same reason—and that is your long-term success. My life became chaotic in the tangle of my sex addiction. My wife felt betrayed by my porn viewing, and she realized that I was no longer the man who had promised to love her—and her alone—for life. Instead she felt she was competing with other women for my attention. Images of women from pornography haunted my mind; I lusted after women I saw on the street, yet I loved my wife and the Lord all at the same time. How could that be? In my sin, everything became weird and convoluted, and I couldn't untangle the mess. Not by myself, anyway. What was happening with me sexually was lust-based, not intimacy-based, and the question was how to start getting back on track.

After lots of prayer, I realized that a time of abstinence, along with my staying away from porn, could allow time for my sexual life to come back into proper focus. My wife was in hiding emotionally, like a turtle all tucked safe inside its shell. I realized that she wouldn't be open with me emotionally or sexually until I could show her consistency in staying pure. I had to allow her whatever time she needed.

Our season of abstinence gave us time to develop true intimacy as a couple. But first, it was important for me to open up to intimacy with the Lord and to be honest with myself so that I could be truly intimate with my wife.

Being in God's Word and staying committed to my accountability partner has been critical to my success. I came to understand—and you need to understand—that this is a complicated process with a lot of moving parts. Be patient. Be persistent.

I see my future relationship with my wife as one of true intimacy—a relationship without secrets and with both of us loving the Lord and each other.

PRAY

Lord, help me to untangle the mess I have made of sex in my life. As I stay away from any sexual activity, draw me closer to you. I can't have a close, intimate relationship with any person until I have that kind of relationship with you.

TAKE ACTION—MARRIED MAN

This rebuilding will take time and a sincere effort on your part. And it is urgent! Every wife needs to see that her husband cares about her in many and varied ways. Become an expert on your wife. Get to know her better than anyone else in your life. List ways you can start to build intimacy with your wife in non-sexual ways.

SINGLE MAN

This devotion can be an encouragement to you to deal with your sexual sin and to start living a pure life—perhaps in preparation for marriage. Know that whatever you are doing now you will take into your future. Marriage cannot cure your purity problem. If you have a flat tire, you'd fix it before you went any farther, right? In the same way, establish your purity before marriage.

Day 73

INNOCENCE RESTORED

Set your minds on things that are above, not on things that are on earth.
COLOSSIANS 3:2

I used to be able to enjoy the company of women without having sexual thoughts. It was fun and simple. I could enjoy them for who they were without any thoughts of sex. However, the use of pornography slowly did something to my brain. Viewing porn methodically ate away at my innocence to the point where sexual thoughts dominated. I would stare and linger over women, dwelling on those thoughts to distraction.

As I delved deeper into sexual sin, my time with women grew more lustful. Thoughts of conquest took over. Instead of enjoying each woman for who she was, I wanted to possess her. I wanted each one to put aside the man in her life and want me instead. Porn teaches you a lie that all women want you sexually.

I began to miss my ability to be innocent with women and just enjoy their company. This thing called porn had robbed me, and I wanted my innocence back. Nobody warned me about this side effect of porn, a hidden cost of the addiction. In fact, nobody ever warned me about porn at all.

In the process of healing, I have learned a technique to break the cycle of lust. When a spiral of lust for a woman started in my mind, I could defuse it by talking with her. Talking to the real person instead of indulging in a fantasy would cancel the thoughts running wild inside my head. Talking to her helped me reclaim some innocence.

As you become more and more free from addiction, You'll regain some of that innocence. It takes time, but have hope; and keep looking forward to victory as porn's grip weakens every day.

PRAY

Lord, restore the innocence that I once had and so foolishly traded for porn. Help me to heal and to keep the same promise that Job made—to covenant with my eyes not to gaze lustfully at women.

TAKE ACTION—MARRIED OR SINGLE MAN

What are the costs of sexual addiction that you did not know ahead of time? List them.

_____

_____

_____

What things were you robbed of that you want to get back?

_____

_____

_____

How are you doing on getting your integrity back? What steps are you taking?

_____

_____

_____

TALKING TO MOUNTAINS

*And Jesus answered them, "Truly, I say to you, if you have
faith and do not doubt . . . even if you say to this mountain,
'Be taken up and thrown into the sea,' it will happen."*

MATTHEW 21:21

I will pray a big prayer, believing that the God who created the universe—
who has counted every hair on my head—can do big things. My sexual
addiction, which is so big to me, is not too big for Him.

I believe that God cares about each of us and wants fellowship with us. He
wants fellowship with me. I believe that the Bible is true. I believe in the resurrection power of Christ. I am going to pray Matthew 21:21, and I will say
to my mountain of sexual addiction, "Go, throw yourself into the sea" (NIV).
I pray this in Jesus' name, and I believe it will be done, just as Jesus said.

Even though I am in the midst of my journey and I'm still learning how
to be free, I am going to believe God's Word. Even when I don't feel it, or
think I can get free, I am thanking God that my addiction has been removed
and thrown into the sea. I need to understand the hurts and pains of the
past that are drivers behind my getting into this addiction in the first place.
There is a need for healing of these wounds, which will take time.

PRAY

Lord, thank you for your resurrection power. Thank you in
advance for lifting me out of my sexual addiction so that I am
not ashamed to have intimate fellowship with you. Lord, help
me to stand firm while I continue to heal. As I study more
about who I am in Christ, about my childhood, please bring
healing to the wounds of the past that are at the root of my
addiction. Help me to be patient with the time needed to heal.

TAKE ACTION—MARRIED OR SINGLE MAN

Make a list of the answered prayers you have experienced recently—and as far back as you can remember. If you have not been a praying man up until now, I encourage you to start right away.

_____

_____

_____

_____

If you have not done so, start a notebook to record your prayers and their answers. You will likely be amazed at how God has been answering you for years. Hopefully this will be an encouragement; God has answered your past prayers—and you can be confident He will answer your future ones.

_____

_____

_____

_____

Do you believe with all your heart that the Bible is true and God loves you? If you haven't yet asked Jesus to be the Lord of your life, today is the perfect time to do it. He's been waiting, you know.

Day 75

WEAKNESS AND STRENGTH

*But he said to me, "My grace is sufficient for you, for my power is
made perfect in weakness." Therefore I will boast all the more gladly
of my weaknesses, so that the power of Christ may rest upon me.*

2 CORINTHIANS 12:9

In the depths of my addiction, I felt very weak and far from God. I was embarrassed to go to Him because of the shame that made me feel unworthy of approaching Him. My weakness felt like a liability, as if it were somehow unique to me; and it separated me from God and others.

However, as I have continued to heal and get into the Word of God, I see that weakness is not a liability at all. The Bible is full of weak people who ended up doing great things. I'm in good company and proud to be one of them.

For example, look at Paul's situation in 2 Corinthians, where he sought God about the thorn in his flesh. The Lord responded to him, "My grace is sufficient for you, for my power is made perfect in weakness." Paul replied, "Therefore, I will boast all the more gladly of my weaknesses, so that the power of Christ may rest upon me" (2 Corinthians 12:9).

This verse makes me realize that my weakness in my sexual addiction did not make me unworthy to approach God. Neither does yours. He holds the promise of my healing. God wants to work in my weakness to show His power for His glory. In other words, He wants the glory for my healing—and yours.

With that knowledge, I understand that I am not struggling only until I can be strong enough on my own. I will never be strong enough to stay pure in my own strength. I accept and rejoice in my weakness and my dependence on God's strength.

As David stood before Goliath, I stand before the addiction—focused on how big my God is and not how big the addiction once seemed. The addiction does not stand a chance against my God.

God wants fellowship with me, and He wants to show His power by overcoming the addiction that I cannot overcome on my own. My God—our God—is great. Great and mighty is He. God wants to restore fellowship with me—and you.

PRAY

Lord, you said that your power is made perfect in weakness. Your Word says that in my weakness, you show your strength. Help me embrace my weakness as the place where you can demonstrate your strength. Thank you for wanting fellowship with me and being willing to reveal your power by using it to overcome the addiction.

TAKE ACTION—MARRIED OR SINGLE MAN

Reflect on David going up against Goliath; a mere boy against a giant who had brought fear into entire armies of men. What was David's strength? He understood that his God was bigger than the giant, and that the giant did not have a chance against his God.

There is no need to be ashamed of your weakness, for through it, God will show His strength. Memorize today's verse, 2 Corinthians 12:9.

Day 76

APPROPRIATE SEXUAL ENERGY

*Husbands, love your wives, as Christ loved the
church and gave himself up for her.*

EPHESIANS 5:25

When I was in the midst of my deepest addiction, my sexual energy was directed at women in porn videos, women walking down the street, women at the gym, women at the office . . . all over the place.

By the time evening arrived, there was not much sexual energy left for my wife. Even then, with what little energy I did have, I might hold off until my wife was asleep—and spend the rest of my energy on porn.

Now, as I am healing, I keep my focus on my wife. God has given me a wonderful woman, and I am putting all my sexual energy toward her. As I stay away from porn and view women in my life in a healthy way, I am able to focus on her exclusively. Because of that, my wife and I are building intimacy daily.

The process of building intimacy takes time and patience. Don't expect instant results.

PRAY

Lord, when I face sexual temptations today, give
me strength to turn away from them. Help me
to focus my sexual energy appropriately.

TAKE ACTION—MARRIED OR SINGLE MAN

Develop your Purity Protection Plan. Your Purity Protection Plan is simply thinking through your day ahead of time. Plan what you will do when you run into situations that have led to sexual sin in the past. In your mind, practice carrying out your plan for each circumstance. This is called mental rehearsal, a technique used by professional athletes to prepare for going up against the opposition.

When you have a plan and practice that plan, you will know what to do when a situation arises. See *Purity Protection Plan* in the Appendix.

MARRIED MAN

Make a list of the typical situations arising during your day that distract you from keeping your sexual energy focused on your wife, and plan how to handle each situation.

_____

_____

SINGLE MAN

As a single man without family responsibilities, you may have more free time. Because of that, you may need a more extensive plan than the typical married man. Adding structure to your schedule—more time planned with mentors, friends, and church activities—would be a good way to start.

_____

_____

Day 77

FACING CONFLICT

Count it all joy, my brothers, when you meet trials of various kinds.

JAMES 1:2

I have learned to face conflict and raised voices head-on instead of clamming up, running away, or cowering. As a child, I was defenseless against adult conflict, loud voices, and angry confrontation. In fear, my reaction was to quietly go off to a secret, isolated place—figuratively and literally.

As an adult, I must deal with conflict. I now face it confidently and work to find a peaceful resolution. If another uses a raised voice during a disagreement, I will calmly ask for a normal tone of voice; and I will offer the same.

As long as there are people involved, there will be differences of opinion. Conflicts will arise, and I need to find ways to work through them in a calm and orderly fashion. I must keep in mind that conflict is not a bad thing, and I will continue to grow and mature as I learn to better handle it in a healthy manner.

PRAY

Lord, I admit that I struggle with handling
conflict. Give me confidence to navigate through
conflicts, remembering to be kind to all people.
Help me to see trials as opportunities to grow
in my reliance on you and your strength.

TAKE ACTION—MARRIED OR SINGLE MAN

Did anything in your childhood cause discomfort with conflict and people raising their voices? Write it down and then answer the questions below.

_____

_____

_____

Did your parents fight? Was either of them a drinker or drug user?

_____

_____

_____

How do you feel when you think back on conflict in your childhood?

_____

_____

_____

What was your typical way to deal with it then? How do you deal with it now?

_____

_____

_____

Develop a plan for how to address future conflicts before they happen.

Day 78

NO FEAR OF ABANDONMENT

I will not leave you or forsake you.

JOSHUA 1:5

When I was ten years old my grandmother died. I was shocked that someone in my close family had passed away. Her death introduced the reality that I could be left alone.

Along with this realization, I really could not understand why, after the funeral service at church, we all went to a bar where a wild drinking party started with much laughter and fun. *Weren't they supposed to be mourning my grandmother?* I certainly felt empty from the loss so the situation at the bar was confusing for me. And then it occurred to me. *What if my parents died?* It was a root fear appropriate for a child, and it led to developing a fear of abandonment.

Even though I was never actually abandoned as a child, in adulthood I recognized that fear operating in my marriage. I often worried when we raised our voices or quarreled. *Will she leave me over this issue? Will I be abandoned?* I was willing to do anything to hold on to the relationship and avoid the dreaded disagreements.

Disagreements are a normal part of a marriage relationship, and I am still learning not to fear a healthy argument. My wife has assured me that she will not leave me over such a dispute, and that I need not fear it. We are two different people, and we will sometimes disagree. And that's okay.

Along with fearing that my parents would leave me, I also feared that God would reject me if I sinned too often or too greatly. But God said He would not abandon me either. As a believer in Christ, I can now accept the assurance of God's Word.

PRAY

Lord, help me to heal from the fears of my youth. Give me the peace that comes from knowing you will never leave me. Help me to remain calm and work through disagreements.

TAKE ACTION—MARRIED MAN

Have you experienced fear of abandonment? If so, explain your fear in several sentences.

Think about having arguments with your wife. Do you have a fear of abandonment in your marriage? If so, write about it.

Will you do anything to make peace? If so, write down a more healthy approach to take.

What have you discovered to be your root fear?

SINGLE MAN

Think about when you have an argument with a friend or girlfriend. Do you fear that your relationship will be lost over the argument? Explain the fear in a few sentences.

Day 79

HELP WANTED

See what kind of love the Father has given to us, that we should be called children of God; and so we are. The reason why the world does not know us is that it did not know him.

1 JOHN 3:1

Now that I have a wife and children, I realize that I have little idea of what "normal" is! I don't want to repeat the dysfunction that I witnessed in my parents. I am actively seeking help. I'm seeking mentors and support, and I am not afraid or ashamed to admit that I need help.

My mom and dad both worked, and my sister and I were busy with our friends. When it was dinnertime, my dad was exhausted and drank too much; and my mom was very impatient with his behavior. I remember her yelling and pouring the contents of booze bottles down the sink. Our dinner table was often like a war zone. I surely don't want my family to live like that.

Over time, I also decided that I cannot drink. I associated alcohol with the chaos of my childhood, and I drank for all the wrong reasons. I drank because I had a rough day at work, or to escape conflict. It was not just social drinking. I will never forget my six-year-old stepson saying to me one evening, "No beer, Daddy." In that moment I realized that he did not like who I was when I drank, just as I hadn't liked who my dad was when he drank. That hit me hard. And it helped me to change.

In the course of our family activities, I sometimes get to a certain point and then I think, *Now what do I do?* Okay, I think that often, not just sometimes. I'm still learning what normal is from other families, and from marriage studies, group Bible studies, men's groups, and mentors.

I am so grateful for getting to know my heavenly Father through the church, other Christians, and the Bible. He provides perfect fathering and perfect love. He is always there for me, and He is not chaotic.

PRAY

Lord, thank you for being my Father, my heavenly Father. I pray for your guidance. Thank you for your Word. Thank you for my earthly father. He did the best that he could and loved me as best as he knew how. Help me as I lead my family.

TAKE ACTION—MARRIED MAN

As you think about your role as a husband and father, where do you need some guidance? Make a list.

_____

_____

What behaviors of your parents have you sworn not to repeat in your own family?

_____

Are you taking appropriate action steps to ensure you don't repeat those parent behaviors?

_____

SINGLE MAN

If you came out of a dysfunctional family, you may not know what normal life is either. Your model for healthy living was broken. Your father may have given you inconsistent love, but our heavenly Father's love is consistent. What steps are you taking to have healthy Christian role models? Do you have a mentor? If not, who can you ask to be your mentor?

_____

If you are a single dad, where do you need some guidance? Make a list.

Day 80

MEETING NEEDS

Steadfast love surrounds the one who trusts in the Lord.

PSALM 32:10

I am no longer in that place where my needs were not met . . . that place in my childhood where I learned that I had to meet my own needs, because the adults in my life were unable to do it. When I was a child, my parents were not always there for me emotionally. Out of that experience, I believed the lie that no one cared about me—that I was unworthy of love. I even felt unworthy of God's love. From that came the thought that if I honestly opened up to God and to people, I would be let down again.

I am learning to accept the love of God. When I seek out God's love, He is right there for me. My family cares about me. My wife meets my sexual needs, and I no longer believe the lie that I have to isolate and meet those needs with pornography. Now I can love and be loved in a healthy, balanced way.

PRAY

Lord, help me to let you love me as I know you do. Help me to trust my loved ones to love me and understand my needs. You are ultimately all I need.

TAKE ACTION—MARRIED MAN

Plan to discuss your sexual needs with your wife in an open conversation. Be sure it is a two-way discussion so you learn what her needs are as well.

How will you get the conversation started?

_____

How has God met other needs in your life recently?

_____

How has He answered prayers?

_____

_____

SINGLE MAN

Your friends care about you and will be there for you if you allow them to be close. As the Bible says, your sexual desires need to wait until marriage; but the love of Jesus is there for you now. Experience the depth of that love, and His grace will be sufficient for you. Jesus is ultimately all you need.

How has God met the needs in your life recently?

_____

_____

List answered prayers.

_____

_____

Day 81

PEACE AND HARMONY

And the peace of God, which surpasses all understanding,
will guard your hearts and your minds in Christ Jesus.

PHILIPPIANS 4:7

My childhood was anything but peaceful and harmonious. With Mom yelling at Dad and Dad's drinking problem, there was always a level of chaos and uncertainty. Would dinnertime hold a measure of peace—or a battle? I never knew what to expect.

While I didn't know it at the time, the perpetual uncertainty was setting me up to look for chaos and excitement in my adult life. I was unhappy in my quiet, uneventful career in a hospital environment and opted for a sales job instead. It was exciting, and unpredictable. Would I be rich at the end of the month—or wonder how we'd pay for the groceries? Sales meant staying up late; working Saturdays; and living on fast food, coffee, and junk from the vending machines.

The lifestyle was oddly comfortable, based on the craziness of my youth. Even so, I complained bitterly. Of course, I didn't realize at the time that this was not the way to live. But it was familiar—so I accepted it anyway.

I am finally learning to enjoy peace and harmony. A number of years ago I got out of sales, and now I enjoy the end of the month instead of dreading it. My income is steady and predictable. I am enjoying a peace that only the Lord can provide—a peace beyond understanding.

With my weekends free, I enjoy getting out and riding my bicycle, taking walks, and eating healthy food. No more diet soda and candy bars for me. Being healthy and happy is my new way to live. I am embracing it and thanking God for it.

PRAY

Lord, thank you for your peace. Thank you for
helping me to understand my chaotic past and
choose to follow you. Thank you for the healing
you have brought into my life. Thank you for loving
me even when I was running away from you.

TAKE ACTION—MARRIED OR SINGLE MAN

What are some of the chaotic characteristics of your life? List at least five.

1. _____

2. _____

3. _____

4. _____

5. _____

In your journal, reflect on what you are doing currently regarding your health and peace.

_____

_____

_____

What are some of the ways you want to improve your health and level of peace?

_____

_____

Day 82

ENJOYING LIFE

Joyful are people of integrity, who follow the instructions of the Lord.
PSALM 119:1, NLT

Sexual sin has felt like the weight of the world on me all day long, every day. Sometimes I have imagined myself like the mythical Sisyphus, pushing the rock up the hill all day, only to watch it roll down and having to start all over again.

But now . . . I will rest in the Lord. I will concentrate on what I can do something about, and not worry about the rest. One thing I can do is reduce the isolation. Going to lunch with friends energizes me in a way that pornography never could. When I meet with a friend whom I haven't seen for a long time, I wonder why I haven't done this more often. Taking my wife to a play or the opera makes me so much more connected to her—and less likely to seek false connection through porn.

I will keep reaching out to get together with godly friends. If someone can't meet, I won't take it as a personal rejection—which, in the past, has led me to isolate. Instead, I will try again. I realize that others are busy, but that they appreciate my effort to reach out for a fun activity.

Jesus had fun, you know. His first miracle occurred at a wedding party. But He didn't just attend the party. He turned many gallons of water to wine so the party could continue. The master of the feast even commented to the groom, "You have kept the good wine until now" (John 2:10).

A wedding celebration was no small party in those days. It might last up to seven days. I celebrate my freedom from sexual sin daily; and I enjoy life far more than before.

PRAY

Lord, I have been so ashamed and isolated in the heaviness of my sin that I have had no joy. Lord, thank you for loving me through this time of healing. Thank you for being the lifter of my head so I can see the beauty of your creation. Help me to find joy as I dedicate my life to serving you.

TAKE ACTION—MARRIED OR SINGLE MAN

If you had all the time that it took, what would you like to do to experience true joy?

_____

Define what is robbing you of your joy.

_____

What can you do to change that?

_____

Write out how finding your freedom in Christ will help you start experiencing joy more fully.

_____

_____

_____

_____

Day 83

BORING IS GOOD

The Lord is my strength and my song; he has become my salvation.
PSALM 118:14

I've learned that I don't have to be super busy every minute of my waking hours. After I check my e-mail, it is unnecessary to look at five different news sources and sports websites, check my fantasy football team, post on Facebook, tweet about something . . . hold it!

What was I doing?

I used to think I had to be in the nightclubs a few nights a week. I sought excitement at every turn. I thought being at home on a Friday night was so dull as to be completely unacceptable. But now? My appointment schedule isn't full from 7:00 a.m. to 11:00 p.m. Monday through Friday.

After I check e-mail in the evening, I turn off the computer and talk to my family. In setting aside the busyness, I now take time for Bible reading. I am able to relax and enjoy a slower flow of activity.

I can be productive without being frantic. I am learning to plan and accomplish what is most important. Yes, carpe diem, but I will take time to smell the flowers; that is part of seizing the day too. I will rest in the Lord.

My new motto is this: *Boring is good.*

Things don't have to be exciting all the time.

PRAY

Lord, help me to rest in you and balance my days
between work, worship, and relaxation. Thank you
for freeing me from the frantic life I used to live.

TAKE ACTION—MARRIED OR SINGLE MAN

What do you want to accomplish that you are not getting done?

_____

_____

_____

_____

_____

_____

_____

_____

_____

_____

_____

_____

_____

_____

_____

In your journal, plan how to manage your day to balance your schedule. For one week, list your activities from morning to night. Take a hard look at how you are spending your time. Make a plan to simplify your week so you accomplish the truly important items. And remember to smell the flowers.

Day 84

JOBS AND PURITY

*And my God will supply every need of yours according
to his riches in glory in Christ Jesus.*

PHILIPPIANS 4:19

I deliberately picked sales—a job full of uncertainty and stress. I often dreaded the end of the month with my income next to nothing one month and crazy high the next. The unpredictability mirrored my chaotic childhood home. Being a salesman drove me to seek out unhealthy coping mechanisms—an excuse for self-destructive behavior that began when I was a boy.

I took a hard look at every aspect of my life—especially where I spent eight hours or more daily—to make my whole life more healthy and godly.

Ultimately, I had to give up my sales job as part of establishing a pure lifestyle.

PRAY

Lord, help me to trust that you are Jehovah Jireh, that I can depend on you to be my provider. I trust that you will provide for my family's needs; it is not the company where I work that is my provider. Help me to take an honest look at my work life and make changes if necessary. I trust that you want the best for me.

TAKE ACTION—MARRIED OR SINGLE MAN

I challenge you to analyze your work situation. A career move could be critical to your long-term sexual integrity.

What attracted you to the job or career field you are in now?

_____

_____

_____

_____

_____

_____

_____

_____

_____

_____

_____

_____

If this job causes stress that leads to sexual sin or otherwise cuts you off from your family, make a plan to change it. This will be a critical part of getting—and keeping—your sexual freedom.

Day 85

LIVING JOYFULLY

I hate the double-minded, but I love your law. You are my
hiding place and my shield; I hope in your word.

PSALM 119:113–114

Living a double life was stressful and sad. Putting on the perfect Christian image at church and then living selfishly when I was alone was a hard way to live. There was no real joy in that. My life was about living for my own comfort and convenience—not for the Lord.

I am now living a new life, with nothing to hide. No more living a double life. I am learning to hope again. I am free from the tyranny of sexual addiction. I am laughing and learning to be joyful. Joy does not come from circumstances, but from knowing Christ and living for Him. I enjoy my new freedom in Christ.

PRAY

Thank you for setting me free. Thank you
for bringing joy back into my life. You
have turned my gloom into sunshine.
You are the true and loving God.

TAKE ACTION—MARRIED OR SINGLE MAN

As you are getting free from sexual addiction, what are some of the ways you are experiencing joy in your life? List at least five.

1. _____

2. _____

3. _____

4. _____

5. _____

Day 86

FADING DREAMS

There is therefore now no condemnation for those who are in Christ Jesus.

ROMANS 8:1

Erotic scenes invaded my dreams from the beginning of the addiction. My looking lustfully at women, combined with porn, left my head full of sinful thoughts and images. They continued right into my sleeping time.

Even though I stopped looking at porn years ago, my highly sexualized dreams are still disturbing. Some men who are seeking sexual integrity may be upset by such dreams, seeing them as a failing, even though during the day they experience victory. However, this is not a failing; not one of us can subdue our dreams.

I know from personal experience that your dreams will change as your freedom from porn increases and time passes. Your dreams will change as you look at women simply as people during the day, instead of lusting after them. I had to determine to put all that sexual desire toward my wife instead of other women. As days become weeks, weeks become months, and yes—months become years—your dreams will become less and less sexual in nature.

There is reason to hope. Dreams will return to normal as you renew your mind.

PRAY

Lord, help me not to be discouraged by these dreams. Help me to stay with the program and have faith that you will restore me, including my dreams. Help me to stay focused on drawing closer to you each day.

TAKE ACTION—MARRIED OR SINGLE MAN

As you continue to avoid sexual sin, what type of dreams would you like to have?

_____

_____

_____

_____

_____

_____

_____

_____

Create a good bedtime routine to help with peaceful sleep. Some experts have suggested deep breathing exercises along with reading the Word before bed. Another suggestion is turning off all electronics, including phones and TV, at least a half-hour before closing your eyes to sleep.

Plan out your evening routine.

1. _____

2. _____

3. _____

4. _____

5. _____

Day 87

JOINING THE PARTY

For you were called to freedom, brothers. Only do not use your freedom as an opportunity for the flesh, but through love serve one another.

GALATIANS 5:13

The deeper I was in the addiction, the more shame I felt and the less able I was to face God. The farther away from God I was, the farther away I was from everyone else. My world was shrinking every day.

Emotionally, I was absent.

As I began to heal, I wanted to start connecting better with God and my family. I sought activities to do as a family, sharing life. I also began realizing that God loves me. He loves me, and my sin has been paid for on the cross. Christ died for all of my sins. Now that I am a believer, nothing can separate me from the love of God.

My faith and trust in the Lord keeps growing, and I have picked my head up and put my shoulders back. I am also rekindling my relationships at church, home, and work—and with my neighbors. The addiction had confined me to a dark, cell-like space; but look out! With God's help I am stepping out to face the great big wide world!

PRAY

Lord, open up my world and help me to be connected again with loved ones and friends. Thank you for your reassurance that my sin has not hopelessly separated me from you. Thank you for opening up my world—out of darkness into the light.

TAKE ACTION—MARRIED OR SINGLE MAN

How have you isolated yourself and felt separated emotionally from your family? List five ways.

1. _____
2. _____
3. _____
4. _____
5. _____

What are you looking forward to as you gain more and more freedom from sexual sin? Make a list.

1. _____
2. _____
3. _____
4. _____
5. _____

How are you experiencing God's love?

_____

_____

_____

_____

Give a shout of praise to the Lord!

Day 88

I AM SORRY

Turn from evil and do good; seek peace and pursue it.

PSALM 34:14, NIV

When I was in the depth of my sin, I tried to believe that I wasn't hurting anyone. I was indulging in something I knew in my heart was wrong, yet I lied to myself. *What harm could it cause?* I'd try to justify it in my thoughts. It wasn't until I finally sought help that I could admit it was hurting others.

In time I came to understand that, most importantly, I had sinned against the Lord as it says in 2 Samuel 12:13. Also, I'm still realizing the depth of the pain I have caused my wife by choosing sexual sin over her. I am working to restore the trust and innocence in our marriage and have humbly asked for forgiveness from my wife.

PRAY

I have sinned against you, Lord, and I seek
your forgiveness. Help me restore my marriage.
Give grace to my wife and me as we rebuild a
marriage that is centered on you. Thank you
for giving me such a wonderful woman as my
wife; I am sorry for treating her the way I did.

TAKE ACTION—MARRIED MAN

One night in my small group, every man was crying as each one realized the pain he had caused his wife. You may not understand the depth of that pain yet, but sometime during this process you will. Have you told your wife you are sorry for the pain you have caused? If not, now is the time. It is important for your wife to seek out a group or Christian counselor to help her process the pain and stress you have put on the marriage. Support her in finding the help she needs.

How can you build trust with your wife and others? List five ways.

1. _____
2. _____
3. _____
4. _____
5. _____

SINGLE MAN

Depending on your circumstances, you may or may not have a wife you've hurt. However, you do have a circle of people including family, friends, and co-workers who have been affected by your lust. You've robbed them of your true self. Sexual addiction makes you hollow, unable to give anything to anyone. You're only able to take from them. Make a list that includes family, friends, neighbors, co-workers, and the Lord. Then list ways to bring healing and build trust in those relationships.

_____

_____

_____

_____

Day 89

CRUISIN' INTO TROUBLE

*The body is not meant for sexual immorality, but
for the Lord, and the Lord for the body.*

1 CORINTHIANS 6:13

It's easy to put the car on cruise control and let it run. There's no need to think about pushing the gas pedal, no worrying about going too fast. You've got the cruise set.

I typically drive the same road on my way to church. This road has a speed limit of 35 mph. It is tough for me to keep the car going that slowly. One day I was pulled over by a squad car. After that incident, I started setting the cruise control for 35 mph.

Cruise control can be beneficial, keeping you from getting tickets. It's not so helpful when it comes to sexual sin. That was also on cruise control for me, and I was not giving the sin much thought. After all, that is the way I dealt with life.

When I finally became aware of the consequences of what I was doing and was convicted by the Holy Spirit of the wrong, I was ready to turn off the cruise control. Now I think about how I live very carefully. I praise God for the daily renewing of my mind and for Him helping me to make the right choices.

PRAY

Lord, I want to turn from my sin and take my sexual life off cruise control. I understand that my body was not meant for sexual immorality. I have struggled with this, and I need your strength. Thank you for your love.

TAKE ACTION—MARRIED OR SINGLE MAN

Are you aware of times when your mind is going down a sexual path and you feel things going into cruise control?

Chart the situation when you notice yourself starting down this path. What's happening physically? Emotionally? What's the time of day? The day of the week? If you keep track each time, you will undoubtedly begin to see a pattern. Seeing the pattern can help you gain understanding and make the changes needed for success.

Day 90

THE HIT RECORD

Whatever you ask in my name the Father will give you.

JOHN 15:16, NIV

When I was a teen, my burning desire was to have a hit record—a number one on the pop charts. I prayed that my neighborhood band would be so great that we'd get noticed and then be signed to a record deal. We practiced many hours. We played at dances, parties, and school assemblies—but we were never discovered. We prayed, but that kind of prayer is not what John 15:16 is all about.

No, this passage is about a much different type of prayer. This is the prayer of a friend of Jesus, a man who has been chosen and appointed to go and bear fruit in this world. This is a man who understands that Jesus gave up His life for him. He is a friend of Christ and wants to demonstrate his friendship by doing what Jesus commands. When I was deep in my sexual sin and convicted by the Holy Spirit to change how I was living, I prayed a new prayer. I prayed that I would be freed from the chains of the sinful life I was living and set free in Christ. Now that's what John 15:16 is all about—a prayer that is in God's will, prayed by a man who is a friend of Christ. That is, us praying back to God what he taught us in His Word about being holy and running from immorality.

We can pray this confidently, and the wonderful news is that we have His promise. If we pray for purity in Jesus' name, the Father will answer us.

PRAY

Lord, thank you for giving us such wonderful hope. You have promised us that you will answer our prayers for freedom. Lord, I pray right now for freedom from sexual sins. I repent of my sins and surrender my life to you.

TAKE ACTION—MARRIED OR SINGLE MAN

You have the opportunity to pray for help with regaining your purity—and to pray knowing that your heavenly Father will answer.

Pray for specific things as you continue your purity journey, even as you finish this book. Start with these examples.

- Focusing on your workout at the gym instead of getting sidetracked by the women
- Planning ways to avoid any distracting women at the office
- Keeping pure during time alone at home

Pray through your list and add to it as you go, putting new ideas into your journal.

Holiday Devotions

ENJOYING THE CHRISTMAS SEASON

For everything there is a season, and a time for every matter under heaven.

ECCLESIASTES 3:1

When I began healing, I had to make up my mind to enjoy holidays with my family. The first time going into the holiday season sober and without sexual sin was uncharted territory for me. I had just begun to uncover the deep wounds that drove the addiction to pornography.

That year I knew I needed to avoid extended time—or any time, even—with my childhood family during the holidays. Making that decision reminded me of going home for Christmas when I was in college—and suddenly feeling like a powerless twelve-year-old again. Walking into the door at home, it was as if I suddenly lost the maturity and independence that I had gained in one semester away from the dysfunction.

In that first year of turning away from pornography, I knew I couldn't risk being triggered by the childhood issues that had gotten me into trouble in the first place. My wounds were too raw, my footing too shaky. I didn't want to give up the progress I had made. Instead, I openly discussed the issue with my wife; we decided to spend time with her family—and time with just our own children, in our own home, where we celebrated the Prince of Peace.

I needed to pace myself through the holidays, not setting up unrealistic and stressful expectations. Similarly, unscheduled time had long been a hazard to my purity, so planning out a relaxed schedule and having a Christmas Purity Protection Plan in place was important. In fact, it's a good idea to use this plan for any holiday that causes undue stress.

PRAY

Lord, this is my first Christmas season without porn. Please help me to stay focused on the birth of your Son at Christmas. Give me your strength not to be overcome by my pain, but to turn to you for healing of past wounds.

TAKE ACTION—MARRIED OR SINGLE MAN

Develop a Holiday Purity Protection Plan.

Your first holiday after making a commitment to sexual integrity can be a particularly treacherous one, loaded with triggers of the past. Plan your time.

_____

_____

_____

_____

Plan an exit strategy from family events if you are getting uncomfortable.

_____

_____

_____

_____

Stay in close contact with your accountability partner.

Holiday Devotions

PLANNING HOLIDAY TIME

*If you do what is right, will you not be accepted? But if
you do not do what is right, sin is crouching at your door;
it desires to have you, but you must rule over it.*

GENESIS 4:7, NIV

While the Christmas holidays—holidays and vacations in general—are busy in one way, they can also include a lot of unscheduled time. Unscheduled time is the danger zone for my sexual purity, and the time between Christmas Eve and New Year's Day can seem endless.

Planning time to go to coffee or lunch with my accountability partner and other safe people during the Christmas vacation helps me stay balanced. I will schedule dates with my wife to go to many of the special Christmas concerts and events in the community like *The Messiah* performances, *The Nutcracker*, and tree-lighting ceremonies. Of course, I will plan to be at church to focus on the birth of our Savior—what Christmas is all about.

When my wife plans a shopping trip . . . surprise—I am going too! I will not let my guard down during the holidays or get lazy about my time in the Word each day. I am determined to look back on each holiday with a testimony that I stayed pure.

Making a call to your accountability partner every day from Christmas Eve to New Year's Day will keep you focused on your purity journey. Scheduling your time in advance as much as possible and doing everything you can to avoid being home alone during the holidays will fill the danger zone with healthy activity.

PRAY

Lord, help me to keep my priorities right during
the holidays and vacations. Help me to be a wise
steward of my time and not to be naive about the
need to schedule my time with other people.

TAKE ACTION—MARRIED OR SINGLE MAN

Start working on a plan for the next holiday or vacation well in advance.

_____

_____

_____

_____

_____

_____

_____

_____

_____

Plan to invite friends to your home on the next holiday. Instead of online
shopping, go to the stores with your accountability partner when you are
looking for a present for your wife. Otherwise, go shopping with your family.

Holiday Devotions

MY NEW YEAR BREAKTHROUGH

Never be lacking in zeal, but keep your spiritual fervor, serving the Lord. Be joyful in hope, patient in affliction, faithful in prayer.

ROMANS 12:11–12, NIV

I have an opportunity to start fresh. I will leave the shame that has plagued me in years past. I will not carry the old thinking beyond this day. I don't need a new year to begin my new life. My book—the story of my life—contains blank pages for me to write a new chapter. With God's power, not my own, this year—today—will be when I break free of my sexual sin.

God provides the strength that I don't have. As I stay committed to keep working through the tough issues, difficulties will not cause me to give up, but strengthen my resolve to keep renewing my mind. Whenever I can, I read recovery books, and I share my recovery story. It takes time and effort, but I am committed to walking with Christ as a free man.

Next New Year's Eve, I will celebrate what the Lord has done. By His grace and power, I will walk in greater and greater freedom from the addiction. I will share my testimony and give Him all the praise and glory for it.

PRAY

Lord, with your strength, during the next year I will seek to grow closer to you each day. I will continue to thank you for giving me men to walk alongside me on the journey. With your strength, I will end this year as a man freed from addiction to sexual sin. Thank you, Lord, for caring about me in my time of trouble; I am praising you in advance for how I will be transformed by your grace.

TAKE ACTION—MARRIED OR SINGLE MAN

Now that you are resolved to start fresh, write down your vision for the next year, and how it will be different from any other. This is your year of break-through to freedom in Christ.

_____

_____

_____

_____

_____

_____

_____

_____

What would you like to accomplish in this new freedom? Make a list.

1. _____

2. _____

3. _____

4. _____

5. _____

Start planning your New Year's Eve toast about how God freed you from sexual sin. Praise the Lord! Jot down some ideas in your journal.

Journaling is an important part of processing your purity journey. In order to write, you need to clarify your thoughts and put them into sentences. To do this, you will have to slow down and think. It will help you deal with the changes going on in your life.

Don't be intimidated by the term *journaling*. It just means to write on a regular basis.

Here are some suggestions for writing in your journal.

- Changes that are going on with your relationships
- Victories in your purity
- Specifics about your sexual struggles
- What you are learning in your Bible studies about God, yourself, and purity
- Insights you are gaining from the devotions in this book
- Gratitude
- Feelings—the whole range of feelings you are experiencing

Another aspect of journaling is talking to God in prayer. Think about the Psalms as an example. David poured out his heart to God in the Psalms, expressing his sorrow, his struggles, and his strong faith. Your journal is between you and God, so talk to Him about your life and your relationship with Him.

Finally, your journal is a written record so you can look back on it in the future. You will be grateful to look back and see God's work in your life through it all. You will see His care for you through the struggle, which will give you peace and confidence of His continued care in the future.

Make journaling an important part of your purity journey.

I believe that some radical intervention is necessary to get you started. Know that accountability software, in and of itself, is not a solution to porn viewing or other sexual sin. The software is part of a strategy to disrupt your typical patterns, creating an opportunity to make better choices for yourself.

There are two main types of accountability software.

- One reports your web browsing activity to another person of your choosing.
- The other is a filtering system that blocks you from gaining access to questionable websites.

Reporting Software

Reporting software helps you to stop looking at questionable websites. It does this by reporting your suspect web browsing activity to your accountability partner. Knowing you will be questioned will motivate you to monitor yourself. The software does not actually prevent you from viewing any particular websites.

Filtering or Blocking Software

The filtering system helps you to make the right choices. The weakness of this system is that a computer-savvy guy may be able to get around the blocks. Also, your software package may not include a reporting function.

Each system has its limitations, but I recommend using accountability software—and perhaps both reporting and filtering types—as a critical part of your strategy.

The Need

Living a life of sexual sin drives you into isolation. Having an accountability partner is critical for your journey because you need to share your struggles with a safe man and stop isolating. Your sexual sins lose their power as you talk them through and bring them out of darkness, into the light. Galatians 6:1 is the model of a great accountability partner.

Whom Do I Choose?

Your accountability partner should not be your wife; this person needs to be a man. I am in no way suggesting that you should hide this from your wife. Quite the contrary. Regularly let her know how you are doing, but all the details of your early struggles are likely to cause her to worry and feel insecure. These are the things to discuss with your accountability partner.

Ideal Characteristics

- Walks by the Spirit as stated in Galatians 5:16
- Shows compassion and empathy without shaming you
- Will maintain confidentiality
- Handles sexual matters with spiritual maturity
- Is willing to make time to help you
- Can accept you right where you are, and give you hope for the future
- Possesses both strength and tenderness to confront as well as gently restore you

If you don't know a man like this, I suggest contacting your pastor. Hopefully, he'll be able to connect you with the perfect accountability partner for you.

Game Plan

Inform your accountability partner that you are reading this 90-day devotional. To be prepared for your time together, it would be helpful for him to have his own copy of *Live Pure and Free*. Invite him to review your responses to the daily action items, and discuss the points of each devotion.

Meet regularly with your accountability partner for coffee or lunch. Stay in touch by phone and text. Be honest and transparent with him and show your appreciation for his faithfulness.

GOAL: Your purity plan is a way to create an environment in which you can have a successful, pure day.

PLAN: Your plan is meant to be adjusted daily or weekly to meet the needs of your life.

- List the typical challenges that you will face today.
- List your action plan for dealing with those challenges.

Example of an office-related plan:

SITUATION	PLAN
1. A co-worker wearing a revealing outfit	1. I will bounce my eyes and avoid passing her desk.
2. Male co-workers having a raunchy conversation	2. I will excuse myself and get back to work.

Make the same kind of list for the rest of your day. Adjust the plan if you find that you have forgotten a certain area of your day or left off a common situation.

In your mind, practice carrying out your plan in each of these situations. This is called mental rehearsal, a technique used by professional athletes. There are examples of this in many sports, from golf to skiing. You may have seen slalom skiers in the starting gate moving back and forth, mentally making their way through the gates.

By creating your own Purity Protection Plan, you will finally stop this round of questions when faced with a situation: *Should I? Shouldn't I? What will I do now?* Avoid the regret of saying, *I wish I hadn't.*

Scripture Memorization

Memorizing scripture is critical for your purity. If you're like me, if it's not on your calendar, it's not going to happen. Write out a schedule of verses for yourself, including dates when you will have them memorized.

- Which verses should you memorize? Start with your favorites, followed by the verses in this book.

_____

_____

_____

_____

_____

_____

_____

_____

_____

_____

- Share your schedule with your accountability partner and recite your memorized verses to him.

A Little	MAD	SAD	GLAD	AFRAID
	bothered	down	at ease	uneasy
	ruffled	blue	secure	apprehensive
	irritated	somber	comfortable	careful
	displeased	low	relaxed	cautious
	annoyed	glum	contented	hesitant
	steamed	lonely	optimistic	tense
	irked	disappointed	satisfied	anxious
	perturbed	worn out	refreshed	nervous
	frustrated	melancholy	stimulated	edgy
	angry	downhearted	pleased	distressed
	fed up	unhappy	warm	scared
	disgusted	dissatisfied	snug	frightened
	indignant	gloomy	happy	repulsed
	ticked off	mournful	encouraged	agitated
	bristling	grieved	tickled	afraid
	fuming	depressed	proud	shocked
	explosive	lousy	cheerful	alarmed
	enraged	crushed	thrilled	overwhelmed
	irate	defeated	delighted	frantic
	incensed	dejected	joyful	panic stricken
	burned	empty	elated	horrified
	burned up	wretched	exhilarated	petrified
	outraged	despairing	overjoyed	terrified
A Lot	furious	devastated	ecstatic	numb

CONFUSED	ASHAMED	LONELY	*A Little*
curious	uncomfortable	out of place	
uncertain	awkward	left out	
ambivalent	clumsy	unheeded	
doubtful	self-conscious	lonesome	
unsettled	disconcerted	disconnected	
hesitant	chagrined	remote	
perplexed	abashed	invisible	
puzzled	embarrassed	unwelcome	
muddled	flustered	cut off	
distracted	sorry	excluded	
flustered	apologetic	insignificant	
jumbled	ashamed	ignored	
unfocused	regretful	neglected	
fragmented	remorseful	separated	
dismayed	guilty	removed	
insecure	disgusted	detached	
dazed	belittled	isolated	
bewildered	humiliated	unwanted	
lost	violated	rejected	
stunned	dirty	deserted	
chaotic	mortified	outcast	
torn	defiled	abandoned	
baffled	devastated	desolate	
dumbfounded	degraded	forsaken	*A Lot*

Every book has a journey. I want to thank some of the key people who made this book possible. With just a handful of devotions in hand, I presented them to Brett Waldman at TRISTAN Publishing, who encouraged me with his prayers. He promised to keep praying as the writing continued.

Taking this same small sample with me to the Mount Hermon Christian Writers Conference in Santa Cruz, California, I presented it to author Judy Gordon Morrow, who read it and loved it. It was her suggestion to add Take Action items to the book.

Special thanks go out to Steven Bradley for assisting me in writing the Take Action items for single men. He jumped right in and spent many hours helping me to get it right.

Then there are my purity group leaders who reviewed the devotions during our fall retreat; Bill Harnist, Paul Zunker, Steve Schmidt, Jim Bluhm, and Michael Becker.

I want to thank my first manuscript editor, Scott Noble, who made it presentable.

I can't forget Jim Lumppio who talked purity over coffee at Rustica, where I did a lot of the writing of Live Pure and Free.

Thanks to all my friends at the Minnesota Christian Writers Guild for their input and the knowledge I gained about the writing craft. I also want to acknowledge my critique group for their input; thanks Jim Lau, Wes Schevenius, and Michael Ireland.

Thank you to Brett and Sheila Waldman for believing in me throughout my writing; and now I get to partner with them as the publishers. Thank you to their editor, artists, and designers for the strength of the final book.

Most of all, thank you to the Lord for freeing me from sexual bondage and giving me the words to put into Live Pure and Free. *To God be all the glory.*